A QUALITATIVE ASSESSMENT OF THE IMPACT OF ENTERPRISE IN EDUCATION AND THE DETERMINED TO SUCCEED STRATEGY ON BUSINESSES

Adam Henderson/TNS System Three

Scottish Executive Social Research

2005

The Department of Enterprise, Transport and Lifelong Learning

Further copies of this report are available priced £5.00. Cheques should be made payable to Blackwell's Bookshop and addressed to:

Blackwell's Bookshop
53 South Bridge
Edinburgh
EH1 1YS

Telephone orders and enquiries
0131 622 8283 or
0131 622 8258

Fax orders
0131 557 8149

Email orders
business.edinburgh@blackwell.co.uk

The views expressed in this report are those of the researcher and do not necessarily represent those of the Department or Scottish Ministers.

CONTENTS

EXECUTIVE SUMMARY 1

   RESEARCH CONTEXT 1

   RESEARCH FINDINGS 1

CHAPTER ONE   **BACKGROUND AND OBJECTIVES** 4

CHAPTER TWO   **METHODOLOGY AND SAMPLE** 6

   QUALITATIVE RESEARCH – RATIONALE 6

   BUSINESSES – SAMPLE AND METHODOLOGY 6

   LOCAL AUTHORITIES – SAMPLE AND METHODOLOGY 8

CHAPTER THREE   **MAIN FINDINGS** 9

   OBSERVATIONS ACROSS THE BUSINESS SAMPLE 9

   BUSINESS ENGAGEMENT WITH DtS ENTERPRISE OPPORTUNITIES 12

   LOCAL AUTHORITIES AND DtS 12

   DtS CHALLENGES 14

   EVIDENCE OF BUSINESS ENGAGEMENT WITH DtS 17

   TAKING DtS FORWARD THROUGH COMMUNICATION 20

CHAPTER FOUR   **CONCLUSIONS AND RECOMMENDATIONS** 21

APPENDIX 1   **DISCUSSION GUIDE DTS ONLY** 23

APPENDIX 2   **DISCUSSION GUIDE DTS AND BEFORE** 26

APPENDIX 3   **INTERVIEW GUIDE WITH LOCAL AUTHORITIES** 29

EXECUTIVE SUMMARY

RESEARCH CONTEXT

1. In March 2005 TNS System Three was commissioned to carry out qualitative research to explore businesses' participation in DtS and the impact of DtS on them. This research focussed on a discrete sample from the business community and should be regarded as providing valuable progress report into the initial impact of the DtS strategy from a business perspective.

2. 24 in-depth interviews were conducted with businesses engaged in enterprise opportunities with schools across Scotland. Each interview approximately one hour in duration. The business interviews were conducted across 10 Local Authority areas.

3. The Scottish Executive identified and provided the business sample, which was divided into 2 main groups: 'DtS and before' (14 interviews) and 'DtS only' (10 interviews). The DtS and before group were believed to have been engaged in EinE opportunities with schools since before the launch of DtS. The DtS only group were believed to have been engaged in EinE opportunities with schools only since after DtS launch and not before.

4. 10 Local Authorities were interviewed via telephone. Each interview was approximately 10-25 minutes in duration.

RESEARCH FINDINGS

5. The key findings from the research are shown as bullet points below:

Observations from the business sample

- Commonalities were found across the businesses sample
    - o All Businesses were currently engaged in a wide range of enterprising opportunities with schools. These ranged from work experience placements to relatively novel arrangements with schools such as co-coaching agreements and teacher placements at business workplaces
    - o Businesses believed there were mutual benefits for schools, pupils and businesses to be leveraged through engaging in enterprise opportunities. For businesses these included: giving something back to the community, public relations benefits and internal staff development. For pupils and schools, businesses perceived benefits included: exposure to the business world, active learning and potentially sparking an interest in a new subject area for pupils
    - o Businesses believed that these mutual benefits would ultimately yield economic and societal benefits
    - o Businesses were aware of DtS and its underlying philosophy but were largely unaware of the specific recommendations underpinning the strategy
- Businesses had a clear idea of what enterprise should be – a combination of attitudinal (a 'can do' attitude thinking about a problem in a businesslike fashion) and practical elements (practical knowledge of how to put ideas into practice). Both elements were

considered vital in furnishing young people with the necessary skills and business acumen to succeed in their working life

- The expected difference in the sample (DtS and before vs DtS only) was not realised in the research findings. Whilst the DtS and before group had indeed been engaged in EinE opportunities for a number of years, this was also found to be the case for the DtS only group.

Business perceptions of DtS

- Businesses agreed with the aim of DtS, therefore general perceptions of the strategy were positive
- For some the existence of DtS as a tangible, national strategy meant that they could compare their own organisation's EinE plan to that of the national strategy, thus providing a useful guide
- Some businesses perceived DtS to be a coordinated strategy that involved a variety of agencies including: Young Enterprise Scotland, Careers Scotland, the Local Authority and the Scottish Executive. For these businesses, this perceived multi-agency approach gave DtS a coordinated feel
- Some businesses were aware of high-level Scottish Executive involvement associated with DtS at the time of its launch. This articulated the importance of the strategy to businesses.

Business engagement with DtS enterprise opportunities

- Businesses had been engaged in enterprise opportunities with schools for varying periods of time

- The main difference in the sample groups (DtS and before vs DtS only) was found to be method of first engagement with DtS
    - DtS and before were likely to be first engaged with DtS via a variety of ways including: at the strategy consultation phase by the DtS national team (at the Scottish Executive), through other agencies (such as Careers Scotland) and through Local Authorities
    - The DtS only group were more likely to have been first engaged in DtS via Local Authority contact. This group benefited through Local Authorities acting as enterprise opportunity idea generators, mentors and communication bridges between them and local schools.

Local Authorities and DtS

- All Local Authorities were actively engaged in the implementation of their DtS plans
- Local Authorities were carrying out individualised approaches to the implementation of the DtS strategy as each had differing geographic, social and economic circumstances
- Each Local Authority was confident that they would achieve the national target of 5 partnership agreements per school cluster – a specific DtS target to be achieved by each Local Authority by 2006

- Local Authorities had adopted a variety of ways in which to engage businesses, including: business breakfasts, partnership agreement sign up sessions and face to face meetings with individual businesses
- In general, Local Authorities felt that the Scottish Executive's role was that of providing DtS support. Many Local Authority DtS post holders had contacted the Scottish Executive's DtS team for ideas and guidance around businesses engagement in enterprise opportunities.

DtS challenges

- For some, partnership agreements were welcome as they defined the parameters of the enterprising relationship between business and school, they also articulated the expectations placed on each party
- The formal Partnership agreement format was found to be best used with businesses who had been lightly or sporadically engaged in EinE opportunities with schools
- Partnership agreements were perceived to be of less value to those businesses who had considerable experience of engagement in enterprise opportunities with schools, or who preferred informal, word of mouth arrangements. Indeed, some Local Authorities claimed that some businesses felt that the partnership agreements were unnecessary
- Some businesses regarded partnership agreements negatively, suggesting it as an approach from the Scottish executive around DtS where the emphasis was on signing up sufficient numbers of businesses to meet targets.

- The individuals interviewed in these businesses were largely unaware of communication material from the Scottish Executive around DtS. However, this may be due in part to the timing of the research which coincided with the mail out of a newsletter (*Engage*) specifically aimed at businesses, which may have reached businesses after the interviewing date
    - o Regardless, businesses perceived communications (*Engage* newsletter shown during interview, DtS website) to be more appropriate for businesses not currently engaged with DtS

- Businesses expressed a desire for local and national DtS progress updates as they were largely unaware of any progress being made on this scale

- Businesses agreed that the DtS strategy must be delivered locally

- In terms of measuring the success or otherwise of engagement in enterprising opportunities, businesses cited differing behaviours
    - o Larger businesses were more likely to have better structured means of measurement. One example was a business recording the number of people in the area applying for certain related subjects when leaving school for HE/FE
    - o Smaller businesses tended to rely on informal, ad-hoc ways of rating the success of their engagement. For example, being invited back to participate with a school in the next academic session
    - o Most businesses were unsure how to measure the success or otherwise of their engagement(s).

CHAPTER ONE   BACKGROUND AND OBJECTIVES

1.1   In 2002 the Review Group set up to assess 'education for work and enterprise'[1] produced a report entitled 'Determined to Succeed'. In March 2003, the First Minister and Deputy First Minister announced the response of the Executive.[2]

1.2   The Executive's response was framed as the 'Determined to Succeed' (DtS) strategy. The aim of the strategy is to increase opportunities for schoolchildren by introducing EinE (Enterprise in Education) in schools creating an enterprising culture among all Scotland's young people and thus contributing to economic growth.[3] The engagement of businesses is seen as crucial to the success of DtS.[4]

1.3   The DtS strategy involves all local authority education departments in Scotland and their schools at both primary and secondary level as well as special schools. Local authorities are receiving significant funds to help to deliver the strategy which is being evaluated separately.

1.4   In the autumn 2004 the Scottish Executive commissioned a survey to explore Scottish SME's (Small and Medium Enterprises) attitudes and perceptions of EinE. The report was published on 7th of February 2005. The survey focussed on SMEs and their awareness of DtS, EinE and related topics. It also looked at businesses' attitudes towards engaging with schools and other organisations such as career services.[5]

1.5   In March 2005 TNS System Three was commissioned to conduct research with businesses engaged in Enterprise in Education (EinE) to explore participation in and the initial impact of the business engagement elements of the Determined to Succeed (DtS) strategy.

1.6   This research was designed to explore the relationship businesses have with schools, investigating experiences and knowledge of being involved in EinE and DtS and whether the

---

[1] 'Education for work and enterprise' later came to be known as 'enterprise in education', EinE.

[2] Determined to Succeed, A Review of Enterprise in Education, Scottish Executive, 2002 http://www.scotland.gov.uk/library5/lifelong/reie-00.asp

Determined to Succeed: Enterprise in Education, Scottish Executive Response, 2003 http://www.scotland.gov.uk/library5/education/dtsr-00.asp

Smart, Successful Future for Scots Kids, Scottish Executive Press Release, 18th March 2003.

A Partnership for a Better Scotland: Partnership Agreement, 2003 http://www.scotland.gov.uk/library5/government/pfbs-00.asp

DtS Evidence Report, Scottish Executive, 2002, p23.

National Priorities in Education, Performance Report 2003, Scottish Executive, 2003 http://www.scotland.gov.uk/library5/education/nper-00.asp

Smart, Successful Scotland, Scottish Executive, 2001 http://www.scotland.gov.uk/library3/enterprise/sss-00.asp

Lifelong Learning Strategy, Scottish Executive, 2003 http://www.scotland.gov.uk/library5/lifelong/llsm-00.asp

Reforms are fundamental to shift in learning, Scottish Executive Press Release, September 2003 http://www.scotland.gov.uk/pages/news/2003/09/SEED300.aspx

[3] For general information on DtS, see webpage http://www.determinedtosucceed.co.uk

[4] Recommendations 4-9 in 'Determined to Succeed' mentioned in footnote 2 above.

[5] http://www.scotland.gov.uk/library5/lifelong/eess-00.asp

strategies are having an impact. This research also involved gathering the views of members of Local Authority DtS teams.

1.7 The research can be seen as providing a valuable progress report into the initial impact of the DtS strategy.

1.8 The overall aim of this research was to inform policy, delivery and future commitments to the business engagement elements of the DtS strategy.

1.9 The specific objectives of this research were to:

- Identify whether the strategies the Scottish Executive have put in place are having an effect
- Identify which elements of Scottish Executive strategy are having the greatest effect in terms of the relationship between businesses and schools
- Identify examples of best practice partnerships between businesses and schools
- Explore attitudes, views, experiences and perceptions held by businesses/employers toward EinE and the DtS strategy
- Focus on which activities employers are involved in and gather views on how well the process works, whilst identifying how benefits and challenges are assessed.

CHAPTER TWO   METHODOLOGY AND SAMPLE

QUALITATIVE RESEARCH – RATIONALE

2.1   A qualitative approach was adopted during this study. When the research objectives are such that the requirement is to explore, understand and identify, qualitative methodologies are particularly appropriate as they allow participants to frame their responses during discussion in their own language as opposed to being constrained by a rigid quantitative questionnaire.

2.3   The specific qualitative interviewing technique employed was governed by the audience and length of interview. For businesses the vast majority of the in-depth interviews were conducted face to face, the remainder by telephone.   For Local Authority contacts semi-structured interviews were conducted over the telephone.

2.4   All participants in this study were recruited via contact lists identified and supplied by the Scottish Executive.

BUSINESSES – SAMPLE AND METHODOLOGY

2.5   The qualitative methodology employed with the majority of this sample was face to face in-depth interviews. These interviews lasted approximately one hour in length and were conducted at the interviewee's place of work. Of the 24 business representatives interviewed, 2 were conducted over the telephone and 22 were conducted face to face.

2.6   Businesses the Scottish Executive considered currently engaged in DtS opportunities were interviewed. The Scottish Executive identified and supplied TNS System Three with the sample of contacts.

2.7   All businesses were contacted via letter prior to TNS System Three commencing recruitment procedures. There were approximately 40 businesses contacted, of which 24 were to be interviewed. The letter contained detail about the research and also provided businesses with the opportunity to opt out of the research if they decided that they did not wish to participate.

2.8   The Scottish Executive segmented the sample of business contacts into 2 main groups – 'DtS and before' and 'DtS only'. Both groups were currently engaged in enterprising opportunities with schools. The 'DtS and before' group were believed have been engaged in enterprising opportunities with schools since before the launch of the DtS strategy. The 'DtS only' group were thought to have been involved in EinE opportunities with schools since after the launch of the DtS strategy and not before. The sample of businesses was further segmented by sector (public / private) and location (Local Authority area). The businesses covered 10 Scottish Local Authority areas.

2.9   The sample structure is shown in table 2.1 below.

Table 2.1   Sample structure of businesses interviews

Type	Total Number	Private sector	Public sector	LA areas
DtS and before	14	10	4	6
DtS only	10	8	2	8

2.10   All fieldwork took place over the period 14 March – 24 April 2005[6].

---

[6] Copies of the discussion guides used at this stage of the research can be found at Appendix 1 and 2.

LOCAL AUTHORITIES – SAMPLE AND METHODOLOGY

2.11   Local Authority post holders with specific responsibility for DtS strategy implementation were supplied to TNS System Three by the Scottish Executive.

2.12   The key benefit derived from speaking to this audience was that they could provide an update into the opportunities with businesses that their Local Authority had been engaged with since the launch of the DtS strategy.

2.13   The methodology selected was semi-structured telephone interviews.   These interviews lasted around 10-25 minutes and were designed to be activity updates as opposed to exhaustive, in-depth interviews.

2.14   The 24 interviews with businesses were scheduled across 10 Local Authority areas. Therefore, 10 Local Authority interviews were conducted.

2.15   Contact details of appropriate organisations were supplied to TNS System Three by the Scottish Executive. TNS System Three wrote to each of the Local Authorities informing them of the research study prior to contact and arrangement of an interview time over the telephone.

2.16   All fieldwork took place 24 March – 14 April 2005[7].

2.17   Table 2.2 below displays the Local Authorities interviewed.

Table 2.2   Sample structure of interviews with Local Authority DtS contacts

Number	LA area
1	Edinburgh
2	Glasgow
3	Stirling
4	Western Isles
5	Shetland Isles
6	Aberdeenshire
7	South Lanarkshire
8	North Ayrshire
9	Perth & Kinross
10	South Ayrshire

---

[7] A copy of the semi-structured interview guide used at this stage of the research can be found at Appendix 3.

CHAPTER THREE   MAIN FINDINGS

OBSERVATIONS ACROSS THE BUSINESS SAMPLE

Commonalities

3.1   It emerged that many commonalties existed across the 2 groups in the sample, the 'DtS only' and 'DtS and before' groups. All were aware of the existence of the DtS strategy and its underpinning philosophy.

3.2   In terms of specific knowledge there was very limited awareness of the specific 20 recommendations of the DtS strategy. However for business purposes, such specific knowledge is of limited importance as, as far as businesses are concerned, they are engaging with schools and their pupils as opposed to executing or fulfilling specific constituent parts of DtS strategy.

3.3   Indeed, businesses who had been engaged in enterprising opportunities with schools for several years were unable to name previous Enterprise in Education government strategies, despite their relatively long term and significant engagement with schools.

3.4   Businesses held the attitude that they would be engaged in opportunities with schools regardless of the existence of the DtS strategy. Some expressed the sentiment that involvement with schools was something that they would be 'doing anyway'. Therefore, DtS was not perceived by businesses to be the main reason that they were currently engaged with schools. Many of the businesses were involved in enterprising opportunities with schools for some time before the launch of the DtS strategy.

3.5   At the outset of the study, the Scottish Executive believed that the main difference between the 2 sample groups ('DtS and before' and 'DtS only') would be that the 'DtS and before' group would have been engaged in EinE opportunities with schools prior to the launch of the DtS strategy, whereas the 'DtS only' group would have begun their engagement with schools after the launch of DtS. However, this was not found to be the case.

3.6   As expected the 'DtS and before' businesses had been engaged in EinE opportunities for many years and certainly prior to the launch of DtS. However, both business groups had been engaged, in some form or another, in enterprising opportunities with schools since before the launch of the DtS strategy. Indeed, some businesses from the DtS only group had been engaged in enterprise opportunities for many years. Moreover, some of the DtS only businesses had well established and highly structured EinE policies in place.

Business Perceptions of DtS

3.7   Perceptions of DtS strategy are generally positive. Businesses feel that DtS fits with their own thinking around EinE. Also, DtS is a good fit for those businesses relatively well defined school engagement / EinE policies.

3.8　　Some businesses felt that the DtS strategy acted as a useful check or means of comparison for their own EinE strategy. Also, the existence of DtS meant that there was a tangible nationwide EinE strategy that could be referred to when advocating increased or sustained commitment to business involvement in EinE for the coming year. There was also some satisfaction expressed from businesses over the goals of DtS being very similar to that of their own EinE policy.

3.9　　Businesses believed that DtS was a coordinated, nationwide strategy. There was an awareness that a variety of stakeholders such as schools, Local Authorities, Young Enterprise Scotland and Careers Scotland were all behind DtS and were collaborating in order to deliver DtS strategy.

3.10　　All businesses were in favour of DtS in principle. For businesses, DtS was helping to push EinE up the agenda. There was a realisation that DtS had enjoyed initial high-level political involvement as its launch and this helped to articulate the importance of the strategy.

> *"It puts it on a broader footing. It has encouraged us to be more precise in terms of what we think we can do to help children...developing a relationship with the schools" (DtS only)*

> *"It is really good to get it recognised at a high level in the company...a Scottish Executive initiative ...and this is how we are supporting it. It really helped when I put my proposal together for my manager" (DtS and before)*

> *"I think nationally there has been a major change in the strategy, and I think perception has changed, that there is encouragement of enterprise education in schools. There is clearly quite a lot going on because I have other business colleagues who have been engaged" (DtS and before)*

> *"They seem to have teams of people from education and Careers Scotland...working together on DtS so it does sound like it has...got more focus" (DtS and before)*

The business view on engaging with EinE

3.11　　Businesses realised that engagement in enterprising opportunities yields a variety of benefits for schools, businesses and ultimately Scottish society.

3.12　　Schools, pupils and teachers were thought to benefit from engagement with business in several ways. Engagement brought an awareness of the realities of the world of businesses and practical knowledge of how businesses turn ideas or theory into workable practice. Pupils were perceived by businesses to gain valuable knowledge and experience and businesses felt that exposure to the business world sparked interest in pupils that could potentially influence their future subject and/or career choices. There was also the belief that businesses could offer pupils and schools a form of active learning that could not be presented to pupils by traditional 'text book' school teaching methods.

3.13　　For businesses, perceived benefits included that they felt they were giving something back to the community through engagement with schools. There were also specific, more tangible benefits that businesses could refer to when discussing benefits yielded through EinE involvement.

3.14   Businesses believed that they were helping to redress specific skill shortages that were a cause of concern in the current workforce and the workforce of the future. This was especially true for those businesses involved in industries where a lack of skills is believed to be particularly acute (i.e. physics, maths and engineering). Business also believed that exposure to their businesses may spark an interest in the pupil and therefore aid future recruitment for their businesses if a relationship could be forged at an early stage, although this was not a priority.

3.15   Other specific benefits to businesses included that business staff could complete continuing professional development (CPD) activities through involvement with teachers and/or pupils and this would help with their career development. Also, business felt that through engaging with schools there could be positive public relations (PR) benefits.

3.16   Ultimately, businesses believed that the benefits to businesses and schools / pupils would have a positive effect on Scottish society as a whole.

What is enterprise?

3.17   Businesses believed that enterprise, whilst rather difficult to accurately define, was comprised of both attitudinal and practical elements – therefore it was not enough to have an 'enterprising attitude' without having the know-how to put theory into practice.

3.18   Attitudinal elements included having a 'can do' attitude and being ready / having the courage to try out ideas and take risks. An enterprising attitude also meant having the ability to think differently about business problems.

3.19   Businesses believed that the rationale behind engaging pupils in enterprising activities was not to encourage a nation of entrepreneurs, as this would be both unrealistic and unsustainable. Rather, enterprising opportunities should help to furnish young people with the necessary skills and business insights to succeed in their working life.

> *"Not with the objective that everybody's going to start a business because that's not possible and the economy couldn't stand it...they will take their enterprising attitude with them. An understanding of the business process and some enthusiasm for it ...will strengthen what they do in whatever organisation they get involved in and that's my understanding of DtS"*
> *(DtS and before)*

> *"There are some people who say that what we have to do is to engender in our young people a 'have a go' mentality. That's only part of it. There's no point in having a go if people don't know how to have a go" (DtS and before)*

> *"What are the characteristics of your Richard Bransons...Alan Sugars?...It is a certain determination and single mindedness that perhaps we should be*

nurturing in some way. It's not going to be everybody but you still need...to help support somebody who's like that" (DtS and before)

BUSINESS ENGAGEMENT WITH DtS ENTERPRISE OPPORTUNITIES

3.20   Businesses were engaged in a wide variety of engagement opportunities with schools. This involvement ranged from the more traditional week-long work experience placement, to co-coaching programmes with teachers, long-term pupil placements, teacher placements at business sites, bespoke 'curriculum-friendly' EinE packs, judging enterprise days at schools and hosting project or subject related day trips from schools.

3.21   It is when the method of first engagement between businesses and the DtS strategy is considered that the main difference between the 2 groups comprising the business sample emerges.

3.22   The 'DtS and before' group were likely to have had their first involvement with the DtS strategy when the strategy was being formulated by the Scottish Executive. Indeed, many of the 'DtS and before' had been consulted in person by representatives from the Scottish Executive before the launch of the strategy. The 'DtS and before' group were also likely to have been engaged with other agencies such as Careers Scotland or Young Enterprise Scotland before engaging with DtS.

3.23   Whilst the 'DtS and before' group had also been engaged in EinE opportunities post DtS launch through the efforts of Local Authorities, the 'DtS only' group were most likely to have been first engaged in DtS via this route. Indeed for the 'DtS only' group, the Local Authorities tended to have played a greater role in terms of their engagement with the DtS strategy. For the 'DtS only' group, Local Authorities played an important role in terms of acting as educators about what the DtS strategy meant for them and they also introduced businesses to Local Authorities. The 'DtS only' group also benefited from Local Authority involvement who acted as useful sources of advice and guidance regarding ways in which a business might get involved with schools.

LOCAL AUTHORITIES AND DtS

3.24   Local Authorities, like businesses, were positive about the philosophy underpinning DtS. All Local Authorities included in the research study were confident about achieving the national target of 5 partnership agreements per school cluster.

3.25   Each Local Authority was currently engaged in a highly tailored, localised approach to implementing DtS strategy in their area. This meant that each Local Authority adopted a unique approach toward DtS and therefore there was no standard approach across the 10 Local Authorities. An individualised approach was thought to be the optimal way to implement DtS strategy in each respective area, as each area had its own particular physical, economic and social set of circumstances.

3.26   Across the Local Authorities there was a wide variety of enterprise opportunities currently being undertaken with local businesses. The type of activity was dependent on the particular approach adopted by the individual Local Authority. The opportunities included:

business breakfast meetings with SMEs, partnership agreement introduction and sign up sessions, face-to-face one-on-one meetings with businesses to explain the DtS strategy and targeted information mail outs introducing and explaining the DtS strategy.

3.27   The Local Authorities regarded their experiences when working with local businesses on DtS to be positive. Local Authorities had found businesses to be, in general, receptive to the concept of DtS and there was good evidence of businesses being 'signed up' to partnership agreements with schools.

3.28   However, whilst the formal partnership agreements were regarded as a recognisable and tangible tool by Local Authorities, they were not believed to be an appropriate means of engaging all types of businesses. Some Local Authorities reported a level of dissatisfaction with partnership agreements as they were perceived by some businesses as too formal. This was especially the case for areas where business was conducted on a very informal or ad-hoc manner.

3.29   In terms of their experiences when working with the Scottish Executive on DtS, Local Authorities regarded this is being a fruitful working relationship. In particular, Local Authorities appreciated the advice and assistance that the Scottish Executive had been able to give them when required. The Scottish Executive was regarded as a good source of ideas around how a Local Authority might formulate and carry out their individualised plans for engaging businesses with the DtS strategy.

3.30   Figure 3.1 below illustrates an approach actually adopted by a Local Authority. This approach shows the intent from the Local Authority post holder to use existing business communication networks to disseminate the message of DtS. This example also shows how the post holder aims to have put measures and procedures in place so that the model for enterprise between businesses and schools in the local area is sustainable in the future.

Figure 3.1: an example of best practice from a Local Authority

LA Business Development Officer Fixed term contract until 2006 Raise awareness of DtS and encourage participation Main strategy is to spread gospel of DtS through EXISTING business networks (Rotary clubs, Chamber of Commerce etc) Sets up business meetings, liaises with private sector enterprise organisations who are working with schools Can identify areas of best practice: school appointing in-house Enterprise Development Officer who is charged with identifying opportunities: monthly meetings with LA, Head Teacher and others AIM: to establish a SUSTAINABLE model for enterprise by the time fixed contract at an end	Therefore – intention not to foster a need for 'hands on' LA involvement over the long term Role is to act as a catalyst for engagement activities Conscious to avoid being an extra layer of administration/ bureaucracy

DtS CHALLENGES

3.31   A number of challenges relating to the DtS strategy implementation emerged during the course of the research with both businesses and Local Authorities. This section will discuss each in turn.

Communication

3.32   The type rather than the volume of communication reaching businesses from Local Authorities emerged as an issue of concern for businesses. In general, knowledge about the DtS strategy held by businesses did not extend beyond the overall philosophy underpinning the strategy. Whilst specific knowledge of the recommendations and targets was not desired by businesses, there was a feeling that businesses did not have an appreciation of how the strategy was 'bedding in' since its launch. Therefore, businesses held no appreciation of how successful or otherwise DtS was proving to date.

3.33   Businesses were concerned that they did not know what was happening with DtS either in their own Local Authority area, in neighbouring areas or nationwide. This lack of knowledge regarding progress left businesses with some questions as to the efficacy of their own EinE involvements.

3.34   Businesses wondered why there was no progress update contact from the Scottish Executive regarding the progress of DtS, especially since many of the businesses had received significant contact from the Scottish Executive in the run up to DtS launch.

Similarly, businesses felt that Local Authorities could have provided information about how DtS was being implemented (and to what success) in their area.

3.35   The desire for progress updates expressed by the businesses is perhaps indicative of the difference in pace between the business and education worlds. Those in the business world are perhaps more used to see results in a shorter timescale than expected in the world of education / policy formulation.

> *"I haven't had a school from…[name-of Local Authority]…approach me to be involved in anything to do with DtS. Now whether this Local Education Authority has taken up the DtS challenge I am not sure" (DtS and before)*

> *"I don't really know how it's gone. I talk to other business people…Some have good experiences; some have bad experiences…Taken quite a long time for this thing to bite and get going" (DtS and before)*

> *"There's a sense of fragmentation sometimes, the sort of things that come out, but I always think that's the key things. As I say, sometimes you'll feel that it's not very joined up" (DtS and before)*

Public relations to date

3.36   There was little recall of the newsletter *Engage* sent to businesses in the spring 2005. However, this may be due in part to the timing of the research, as it was also conducted in spring of 2005. Each of the 24 business interviewees was shown a copy of the newsletter. Whilst relatively interesting, the newsletter was thought to be of more use to those businesses who were not currently engaged with DtS. Ways in which the newsletter could be made more relevant to businesses currently engaged included if a progress update was given on how DtS was being implemented across Scotland. Regional progress updates were also cited as desired information for businesses.

3.37   There was little recall of the media campaign aimed at businesses. Although the primary aim of the campaign was to raise awareness of DtS rather than to engage businesses, awareness of the campaign across the 24 businesses was very low. Local Authorities commented that they had not received any enquiries from businesses as a result of the media campaign. Some Local Authority contacts commented that in certain, more rural areas, the best approach to adopt if trying to communicate with businesses was a face to face informal approach.

Private sector involvement

3.38   There were varying attitudes found toward the involvement of the private sector. Some Local Authorities had employed the services of private companies to act as enterprise consultants. These companies assisted the Local Authority with their individual DtS strategies – opportunities included acting as the link between businesses and schools, acting as enterprise idea generators for schools and signing up businesses to Local Authority partnership agreements. Some Local Authorities had decided to adopt this approach as some felt they did not have the appropriate level of knowledge of enterprise and business. Another reason for private sector involvement was that it reduced the workload for the Local Authority (given their finite resources).

3.39   A small number of businesses had reservations around the use of private consultants in this way. These concerns were based around the belief that private companies were profiting from enterprise opportunities with schools as the businesses themselves were giving of their time for free.

3.40   Some businesses intended to promote their own enterprise programmes which have been formulated in line with their own businesses agendas. However well intentioned, it may be that these private business initiatives do not have the education and development of young people as their overriding objective.

Local vs National delivery

3.41   Businesses and Local Authorities accepted that the DtS strategy must be delivered via Local Authorities, due to the unique set of economic, social and geographic circumstances at play for each authority. There was a realisation from Local Authorities and businesses that Local Authorities could not adopt a 'one size fits all' approach to tying to engage businesses in their area.

3.42   For some businesses, the most recent update regarding the DtS strategy they had received was at the time of launch. On a national level, lack of communication meant that the feeling of being involved in a national strategy was being diluted. At a local level, a perceived lack of communication meant that some businesses were unsure as to how they were performing with regard to DtS when compared to other businesses and they were also unsure as to what was happening regarding DtS in their local area.

3.43   A small number of businesses felt that the priorities of the Local Authority meant that their enterprise activity was not considered for inclusion in DtS. These businesses were likely to have their own programmes, or heavy involvement in existing programmes which involved their business engaging with schools. These businesses reported negative experiences when engaging with Local Authorities and the Scottish Executive, mainly due to their enterprise opportunities not matching with the Local Authorities DtS strategy plan. However, it may be the case that such issues are inevitable when individual strategic approaches are adopted.

Formal Partnership Agreement Formats

3.44   Across the businesses, the formal partnership agreement format was found to be most appropriate for those businesses that were either new to EinE, or had previously been relatively lightly engaged in EinE opportunities with schools. For these businesses, the partnership agreement format helped formalise their relationship with the schools and articulate what was expected from both the school and the business. Also, the partnership agreement provided tangible evidence of their involvement with schools.

3.45   For some of the businesses who had been engaged in enterprise opportunities for a number of years, the partnership agreements were regarded as an unnecessary appendage to their engagement with schools. Some felt that they did not require a formalisation of a relationship that had been in existence for some time.

3.46 Additionally, some businesses felt that the process of 'signing up' businesses and schools in this way suggested something of a tick box mentality being adopted by Local Authorities. However, this opinion was by no means held by the majority of businesses. Indeed, some found the partnership agreements as a relatively useful document.

> *"She wanted to formalise the partnerships with the businesses that she worked with. Basically she just asked if that would be ok and we said 'Yes we're doing it anyway. We might as well.' It was very painless!" (DtS and before)*

Measurement

3.47 In terms of measuring the effect of engagement in enterprise opportunities, businesses elicited a variety of views and practices around this topic. Generally, the larger the businesses, the more sophisticated the method of measurement applied. For example, some large businesses measured the effect in terms of the number of people who participated in EinE opportunities with them going on to select a related subject (i.e. physics or chemistry) in further or higher education.

3.48 For smaller scale businesses, measurement of the success or otherwise of their involvement tended to be relatively ad-hoc. For example one business commented that if they were invited back to participate next year by the school, they must be doing something right.

3.49 An overall finding was that most businesses were relatively unsure about how to measure the quality or impact of the enterprise opportunity they had engaged with.

3.50 The issue of measurement, although difficult to define in the context of enterprise, was an important issue for businesses and Local Authorities with regard to DtS. There was a general belief held that as DtS remained a strategy in relative infancy, there was no expectation for accurate or comprehensive measurement and/or evaluation to have been conducted. However, there was a desire from businesses to gain an appreciation or feeling for how DtS strategy was progressing, that it was moving forward and that they remained part of something national and worthwhile.

EVIDENCE OF BUSINESS ENGAGEMENT WITH DtS

3.51 This section will highlight a selection of case studies illustrating examples of enterprise opportunities between businesses and schools.

Figure 3.2   Evidence of DtS influencing the design and roll-out of a multi-national company's EinE strategy

- Multinational company

- Approached initially by Scottish Executive / Hunter Foundation

- Tailored existing national scheme to better fit the requirements of DtS

- Innovative practice: co-coaching / pairing own staff with head teachers

- 'Early days' but plans for expansion of programme

- Engagement yields many benefits:
    - o   understanding of business model for teachers
    - o   appreciation that the worlds of business and education are not that dissimilar!
    - o   opportunity to talk over plethora of issues: enterprise, work/life balance, management of budgets, staff problems, communication within and beyond school.

3.52   Figure 3.2 illustrates how a multi-national company combined its thinking and planning with that of DtS strategy to produce and innovative programme that involves head teachers of schools across Scotland partnering senior business figures to co-coach each other.

Figure 3.3   Evidence of business being dissatisfied with lack of contact with Local Authority

- Well established SME

- Sustained & multiple involvement with schools over 25 years

- Was consulted on the strategy for DtS by the Scottish Executive prior to its launch and is familiar with DtS strategy

- No contact from LA or Scottish Executive since DtS launched and this is surprising – "I have been expecting to have my hand bitten off"

- Lack of information about status quo: unsure about how DtS being implemented

- Can't understand benefit of DtS vs what has preceded it – "My gut feeling…and experience locally is that it hasn't been any better that what went before"

3.53   Figure 3.3 illustrates a well established SME who expressed dissatisfaction with the level of contact received around DtS post launch. This particular SME had been involved at the strategy formulation stage (had received contact from the Scottish Executive) but not since. This had led to a feeling of ambiguity over why there had been such a lack of contact.

Figure 3.4   Evidence of DtS formalising EinE engagement opportunities

- Multinational company

- Engaged in ad-hoc educational activities for several years

- Recently formalised involvement through a DtS Partnership Agreement

  o   "We're already doing it, we may as well recognise that fact."

  o   "It was very painless."

- Current frequency of involvement very high

- Encouraged by increased level of contact from Local Authority and school

- shifts onus from the business – a true partnership.

3.54   Figure 3.4 highlights an example of how a partnership agreement can crystallise enterprise opportunities between schools and businesses. In this case, a business that had been involved in ad-hoc enterprise opportunities with schools for several years was increasing its level of involvement as a result of agreeing enterprising opportunities with the Local Authority and school.

TAKING DtS FORWARD THROUGH COMMUNICATION

Figure 3.5   Communication messages and their potential effect

Message	Effect
• DtS here to stay • Not a political football – DtS has support from apolitical/philanthropic bodies such as the Hunter Foundation • Additional funding has been granted	• Safeguards against scepticism over motives and commitment levels toward DtS strategy
• National and local progress updates • DtS is working • Communicate business meeting opportunities at local and national level	• Maintains interest at top of mind level • Communicates MY involvement is making a difference • Snowballing of ideas – consistent with way in which businesses operate
• Examples of ways in which to engage • HOW best practice examples achieved, not simply WHAT achieved	• Stimulates imagination • Articulates flexibility of DtS • Communicates ease of engagement

3.55   Figure 3.5 shows potential messages that the Scottish Executive may wish to communicate around DtS and, on the right, their potential effect on business attitudes and perceptions around DtS.

> *"Every so often they'll (Barnardos) drop us a note saying 'Here's a list of ten things that we're up to. If you're interested...give us a shout' These are short-term tactical office-based but equally the conversation could be around the planning of a 3 year programme...They are focussing the communication on opportunities that we might want to take, that would be of interest to us, that would fit with our profile" (DtS only)*

> *"Long term strategy...I think that's something that's needing to be clearly communicated" (DtS and before)*

CHAPTER FOUR   CONCLUSIONS AND RECOMMENDATIONS

4.1   In general, businesses hold positive attitudes towards DtS. Businesses are on the whole positive about the philosophy underpinning DtS strategy and believe that enterprise should play a significant role in the lives of young people.

4.2   Through increased, continued or more formalised engagement with schools and through the existence of a national strategy such as DtS, businesses held the perception that enterprise was moving up the educational agenda in Scotland. Indeed the fact that DtS existed as a national strategy created the impression, for some businesses, of a cohesive approach to EinE from the Scottish Executive.

4.3   Through their involvement in enterprising opportunities, businesses believe that DtS is working to some extent. In general, the experiences businesses have had when engaging with schools have been positive. Some businesses expressed concerns over the extent to which teachers understood the business world (in terms of timing commitments of businesses and teachers willingness to work out of their usual hours) however these were minor concerns and were expected to dissipate over time.

4.4   Businesses were open to further suggestions as to increase or develop their engagement with schools and were generally positive about their future relationships with schools. Generally, the businesses were very receptive to new and different enterprise opportunities they could get involved in.

4.5   Through the efforts of Local Authorities facilitating partnership agreements between businesses and schools, there is evidence to suggest that the number of enterprise opportunities is increasing. Local Authorities have been involved in encouraging businesses and schools to enter into partnership agreements and this had been achieved through activities such as business breakfasts and partnership signing ceremonies.

4.6   There is evidence to suggest that the formal partnership agreement format is best suited to businesses who have been lightly involved with schools in the past or who are relatively or completely new to EinE. For businesses with a relatively long history of EinE opportunity engagement with schools some find partnership agreements a rather unnecessary appendage to their informal agreement with schools. Local Authorities should therefore carefully decide upon which businesses to target for partnership agreement signing, or should consider how they introduce these agreements to businesses so they are not met with unnecessary hostility.

4.7   We believe that Local Authorities should be striving to generate and promote a sustainable model for enterprise opportunity engagement between schools and businesses. Eventually, this model should not require input from Local Authorities as the necessary communications and information networks will have been put in place. There is evidence from the Local Authorities to suggest that this model is beginning to take shape.

4.8   We believe there is a strong role for communications to articulate what is happening in terms of DtS on both a national and local level. Businesses are currently unsure as to how DtS is progressing. Businesses also do not know what other businesses are doing in terms of enterprise opportunity engagement. Businesses also wish to know that their involvement is making a difference to young people.

4.9   We believe that communication should be a priority for the DtS team. This communication should specifically target those businesses already engaged in DtS as well as trying to attract new businesses to DtS. We believe that communications inappropriate for currently engaged businesses will have a detrimental effect on business' perceptions of DtS, enthusiasm for EinE opportunity engagement and future business commitment to DtS strategy.

4.10   We believe that communication to currently engaged businesses may be best achieved through face to face meetings, such as business networking events at a local and / or national level. Whilst businesses appreciate that DtS is still in relative infancy, we believe that the Scottish Executive should consider how to further raise the profile of the DtS strategy with the business community.

APPENDIX 1   DISCUSSION GUIDE DTS ONLY

DtS 119154: <u>DtS only</u>: FINAL discussion guide

1.   Research background and introductions (5 mins)
o   Introduce self and TNS System Three
  o   **Independent** research agency. Confidentiality – tape recording. MRS standards.
  o   Interview to last c.1 hour
  o   Purpose of interview: would like to ask them about their experiences with schools and how they view the role of Enterprise in Education in schools. We wish to get detailed feedback on the Determined to Succeed strategy. This will offer the opportunity for businesses to contribute potential improvements to the processes involved.

o   **Introduction**
  o   Nature of business/organisation, size, how long established
  o   Role within business
  o   Role relating specifically to DtS

2.   Relationship with school (20 mins)
•   What types of projects/involvement has your business/organisation had with schools. Explore.

  o   Why involved with schools?

  o   SPONT: how did these relationships begin?
  o   THEN PROBE: How were these set up/organised? How did this work? Explore. Did they match up to your expectations? – better or worse?
  o   Who involved: From business? From school?
  o   How is the relationship managed?
  o   Type of pupil involved with? Age / interests / personality type?
  o   Why not engage before? PROBE: time pressure? Lack of knowledge? Lack of approach by school / Local Authority etc. Discuss.
  o   Would you encourage other businesses to get involved? What ways might we use to encourage more businesses?

  o   Why do you think pupils should be involved in 'enterprising activities' with businesses?
    ▪   Benefits to school / pupil / business? Explore.

•   How successful do you think the experience(s) have been with the school? For both school and your business? SPONT. THEN:
  o   Highs / lows from engaging in DtS with:
    ▪   Pupils / Schools

•   What good does it do? For who? Regarding contacts with pupils? Benefit who? How? Explore.
•   Rationale for above? How know successful or otherwise? How does this feel? Explore.
  o   How do they evaluate the benefits of DtS?
•   Since involved with the school, has this met with expectations? Which areas / features? Explore.
  o   Does it deliver what they were 'sold'? Explore.
•   Any improvements? Features / areas / procedures that would make the process easier?

3.   Determined to succeed - (20 mins)
MODERATOR NOTE: THE INTERVIEWEE HAS BEEN SENT A LEAFLET (engage) BY THE EXECUTIVE AND POINTED TOWARD THE DtS WEBSITE PRIOR TO INTERVIEW.

- Thoughts on DtS. SPONT.

- High / low points of strategy
- Specifics:
    - Probe fully.
- How do they understand the terms "enterprise" and "entrepreneurial activity", themselves, and when working together with schools?
- Where do they see EinE fitting with other more traditional subjects? PROBE: what about in terms of the work-based vocational element of DtS?

- How change / modify / develop / improve strategy? Explore.

NOTE: MODERATOR TO HAND OUT SHEET OF DIFFERENT WAYS THAT THE BUSINESS CAN GET INVOLVED WITH THE SCHOOL (TAKEN FROM PARTNERSHIP TEMPLATE DOCUMENT)

- Thoughts on this? Likely to engage? Which ways? Explore.
- Which category do they 'fit' into

- DtS – how does this work for them? How do they engage with the strategy? Explore.
- What does the DtS strategy mean for them in practice? Explore.
- Thinking about the ways in which one can engage, thoughts?
    - Now?
    - In future?

- Any contact from other people about EinE / DtS? SPONT:
    - Scottish Executive / Local Authority?
    - Explore contact.

- How would they rate the Scottish Executive / Local Authority role in providing leadership & support?

- Awareness of partnership agreement between schools and businesses? (**NOTE:** THIS COULD BE LOCAL / REGIONAL / NATIONAL / Or not at all)?
    - Discuss plan / contract if applicable.

- What think about approach from authorities? How does this work? How does this feel?

4. **Communication and marketing (5 mins)**
- What information received so far? SPONT. THEN:
    - PROBE ON 'engage' newsletter. **NOTE:** MODERATOR TO SHOW INTERVIEWEE COPY IF REQUIRED.
        - Seen before?
        - Thoughts?
        - Thoughts on type of information included. Explore.

    - Repeat above process for website (AND ANY OTHER MATERIAL AS APPROPRIATE)

- What type of information required? SPONT. THEN:
    - Updates on policy
    - New ideas for engaging with schools

- Case studies
- Anything else?

- How wish to be kept in touch?
  - Best channel?

5. The future (10 mins)
- To what extent have they developed a greater understanding of education through DtS/ EinE activities? How.

- In order to develop more enterprise opportunities with the school, how could your business/organisation do this?
  - What would be the best ways in which to do this?
  - Could the school do anything more to achieve this?
  - Can the Local Authority / Scottish Executive do more?
  - Would you require any additional support in order to achieve this?
  - Positive and negative?

  How can more businesses become involved?

- How committed do you feel the school / Local Authority / Scottish Executive is to forging closer links between schools and business. (relationships) To the wider local community? Explore.

- Anything to add?

THANK AND CLOSE

APPENDIX 2   DISCUSSION GUIDE DTS AND BEFORE

DtS 119154: <u>DtS AND BEFORE</u>: FINAL

1.   Research background and introductions (5 mins)
o   Introduce self and TNS System Three
  o   **Independent** research agency. Confidentiality – tape recording. MRS standards.
  o   Interview to last c.1 hour
  o   Purpose of interview: would like to ask them about their experiences with schools and how they view the role of Enterprise in schools. This will offer the opportunity for businesses to contribute potential improvements to the processes involved. **Also** will provide an opportunity to assess impact of DtS strategy given you have been involved in EinE with schools prior to the strategy's launch in 2003.

o   **Introduction**
  o   Nature of business/organisation, size, how long established
  o   Role within business / Role relating specifically to EinE

2.   Relationship with school - (20 mins) NOTE: THESE BUSINESSES WILL HAVE HAD A SIGNIFICANT LONG-STANDING INVOLVEMENT WITH EinE ACTIVITY WITH SCHOOLS
*   Why involved with schools? Explore.

*   Current EinE activity with school / school pupils. Explore.
  o   Type of activity(s)
  o   Length of time involved.

  o   Who involved: From business? From school?
  o   How is the relationship managed?
  o   Type of pupil involved with? Age / interests / personality type?

*   Any change over time / last couple of years? Explore.
*   What previous activities have they been involved in?
*   Awareness of any change in approach / EinE strategy from:
  o   Schools
  o   Local Authorities
  o   Scottish Executive
*   How successful do you think the experience(s) have been with the school? For both school and your business? SPONT. THEN:
  o   Highs / lows from perspective of:
    ▪   Pupil / School / Business

*   What good does it do? For who? Regarding contacts with pupils? How? How do they evaluate the benefits of EinE?
*   Rationale for above? How know successful or otherwise? How does this feel? Explore.
*   Any improvements? Features / areas / procedures that would make the process easier?
  o   From: Scottish Executive / schools / themselves?

3.   Determined to succeed - (20 mins)
MODERATOR NOTE: THE INTERVIEWEE HAS BEEN SENT A LEAFLET 'engage' BY THE SCOTTISH EXECUTIVE AND POINTED TOWARD THE DtS WEBSITE PRIOR TO INTERVIEW.
*   Initial thoughts. SPONT. THEN:

- Knowledge about DtS. Explore.
- Areas of interest / contention etc. Explore.
- High / low points of strategy.
- Specifics:
  o Probe fully.
- How do they understand the terms "enterprise" and "entrepreneurial activity", themselves, and when working together with schools?
- Where do they see EinE fitting with other more traditional subjects? PROBE: what about in terms of the work-based vocational element of DtS?

- **How compare with previous EinE strategies?**
  o CHECK: can name any previous strategies?
- How would you change / modify / develop / improve strategy? Explore.

NOTE: MODERATOR TO HAND OUT SHEET OF DIFFERENT WAYS THAT THE BUSINESS CAN GET INVOLVED WITH THE SCHOOL (TAKEN FROM PARTNERSHIP TEMPLATE DOCUMENT)

- Thoughts on this? Likely to engage? Which ways? Explore.
- Which category do they 'fit' into

- DtS – how does this work for them? How do they engage with the strategy? Explore.
- SPONT. THEN PROBE:
  o 'Fit' of plan / DtS strategy objective with their own plans / processes for DtS?
  o How affect ways in which they approach EinE / engaging with pupils?
  o Thoughts on 'formalising' relationship in this way. Explore.

- Any contact from other people about EinE / DtS? SPONT:
  o Scottish Executive / Local Authority?
  o Explore contact.

- Awareness of partnership agreement between schools and businesses? (**NOTE:** THIS COULD BE LOCAL / REGIONAL / NATIONAL)?
  o Discuss plan / contract if applicable.

- What think about approach from authorities? How does this work? How does this feel?
  o Improvements

4. **Communication and marketing (5 mins)**
- What information received so far? SPONT. THEN:
  o PROBE ON 'engage' newsletter. **NOTE:** MODERATOR TO SHOW INTERVIEWEE COPY IF REQUIRED. ALL BUSINESSES HAVE BEEN SENT THIS.
    ▪ Seen before?
    ▪ Thoughts?
    ▪ Thoughts on type of information included. Explore.

  o Repeat above process for website (AND ANY OTHER MATERIAL AS APPROPRIATE)

- What type of information required? SPONT. THEN:
  o Updates on policy
  o New ideas for engaging with schools
  o Case studies

- o   Anything else?

- How wish to be kept in touch?
   - o   Best channel?

5.   The future (10 mins)
- To what extent have they developed a greater understanding of education through DtS/ EinE activities? How.

- How do you perceive your involvement in EinE in future?

- In order to develop more enterprise opportunities with the school, how could your business/organisation do this?
   - o   What would be the best ways in which to do this?
   - o   Could the school do anything more to achieve this?
   - o   Can the Local Authority / Scottish Executive do more?
   - o   Would you require any additional support in order to achieve this?

   - o   How committed do you feel the school / Local Authority / Scottish Executive is to forging closer links between schools and business. To the wider local community? Explore.

How could more businesses become involved?

- Anything to add?

THANK AND CLOSE

APPENDIX 3   INTERVIEW GUIDE WITH LOCAL AUTHORITIES

119154 – Semi-structured interview guide with Local Authorities – Determined to Succeed (DtS): FINAL

Note: each of the areas interviewers will cover. However, this guide should be viewed as fluid in that the interviewee will phrase responses in their own language, and will be encouraged to raise points they feel are salient. Interview length – 10 minutes.

Each interviewer will have read the Local Authority plan prior to interview and will be aware of the key recommendations of the DtS strategy, specifically those that relate to business.

Note: each business will have received a letter from TNS System Three explaining about the research with businesses and also our intention to contact them

READ OUT: WE ARE CONDUCTING RESEARCH WITH BUSINESSES IN YOUR AREA ON BEHALF OF THE SCOTTISH EXECUTIVE ABOUT THEIR INVOLVEMENT IN ENTERPRISE IN EDUCATION (EinE) GENERALLY AND THE DtS STRATEGY SPECIFICALLY. THE SCOTTISH EXECUTIVE HAS GIVEN US ACCESS TO YOUR LOCAL AUTHORITY PLAN WHICH EXPLAINS YOUR AUTHORITY'S PLAN WITH RESPECT TO IMPLEMENTING THE DtS STRATEGY. THE PURPOSE OF THIS INTERVIEW IS TO GET A BRIEF UPDATE ON WHAT HAS HAPPENED BETWEEN YOUR LOCAL AUTHORITY AND BUSINESSES IN THE LAST 12 MONTHS OR SO. THIS CONVERSATION IS ENTIRELY CONFIDENTIAL.

Question 1
PLEASE TELL ME WHAT YOUR ROLE IS WITHIN THE LOCAL AUTHORITY IN TERMS OF ENTERPRISE IN EDUCATION ACTIVITIES WITH BUSINESS

Question 2a
PLEASE EXPLAIN TO ME YOUR LOCAL AUTHORITY'S PLAN REGARDING IMPLEMENTING THE DtS STRATEGY WITH BUSINESSES.

Question 2b
HOW HAS YOUR LOCAL AUTHORITY PLAN TOWARD ENGAGING WITH BUSINESSES AND EinE CHANGED SINCE THE ARRIVAL OF THE DtS STRATEGY (PROBE for what was in place before if anything)?

Question 3a
IN TERMS OF DtS: WHAT TYPES OF ACTIVITIES HAS YOUR LOCAL AUTHORITY HAS BEEN INVOLVED IN WITH BUSINESSES OVER THE LAST 12 MONTHS? (Note: these could be seminars / training days / open days)

Question 3b

HOW SUCCESSFUL HAVE THESE ACTIVITIES BEEN (probe for any problems / difficulties)?

Question 3c

HOW DO YOU MEASURE THE SUCCESS OF DtS ACTIVITIES WITH BUSINESSES?

Question 4

TELL ME HOW YOU THINK YOUR LOCAL AUTHORITY'S RELATIONSHIP IN TERMS OF DtS WITH LOCAL BUSINESS COULD BE IMPROVED?

Question 5

HOW DO YOU ENVISAGE THE ROLE OF LOCAL AUTHORITIES IN A LEADERSHIP CAPACITY IN RELATION TO IMPLEMENTING DtS

Question 6a

WHAT LEADERSHIP HAS THE SCOTTISH EXECUTIVE PROVIDED?

Question 6b

CAN YOU SUGGEST ANY IMPROVEMENTS TO THIS LEADERSHIP?

Question 7

IS THERE ANYTHING ELSE YOU WOULD LIKE TO ADD?

THANK AND CLOSE

RESEARCH - PUBLICATIONS LIST FROM 2002

An Evaluation of Section 18 of the Mental Health Implementation of Part 5 of the Adults with Incapacity (Scotland) Act 2000: Julie Ridley, Lyn Jones, Anne Robson, Scottish Health Feedback. (2002) (£5.00)
Summary available: Health and Community Care Research Findings No.18

Routes Out of Homelessness: Ann Rosengard, Isla Laing, Alice Ann Jackson and Norma Jones (Ann Rosengard Associates). (2002) (£5.00)
Summary available: Development Department Research Findings No.131

Researching Women in Rural Scotland: Elaine Samuel. (2002) (£5.00)

Gypsies/Travellers in Scotland: The Twice-Yearly Count - No.1. (January 2002) (Free)

Providing Free Personal Care for Older People: Research commissioned to inform the work of the Care Development Group: edited by Diane Machin and Danny McShane. (2002) (£10.00)
Summaries available: Health and Community Care Research Findings Nos.3, 4, 5, 6, 7 and 8

Neighbourhood Management: Lessons from Working for Communities Pathfinders and related initiatives: Alison P Brown. (2002) (£5.00)
Summary available: Development Department Research Findings No.132

Towards a Plan for Action on Alcohol Misuse: Responses to the Written Consultation: Reid Howie Associates. (2002) (£5.00)
Summary available: Health and Community Care Research Findings No.10

Towards a Plan for Action on Alcohol Misuse: Summary of Evidence: Reid Howie Associates. (2002) (£5.00)
Summary available: Health and Community Care: Research Findings No.11

Attitude Towards Alcohol: Views of the General Public, Problem Drinkers, Alcohol Service Users and their Families and Friends: Becki Lancaster and Anna Dudleston. (2002) (£5.00)
Summary available: Health and Community Care Research Findings Nos.12 and 13

Consultation with Children and Young People on the Scottish Executive's Plan for Action on Alcohol Misuse: Kathryn Potter. (2002) (£5.00)
Summary available: Health and Community Care Research Findings No.14

International Alcohol Policies: a Selected Literature Review: Kate Sewel. (2002) (£5.00)
Summary available: Health and Community Care Research Findings No.15

Public Attitudes to the Healthcare of Older People in Scotland: Simon Braunholtz and Barry Stalker. (2002) (£5.00)
Summary available: Health and Community Care: Research Findings No.16

Legal Studies Research Programme 2002: Legal Studies Research Branch. (2002)

Biodiversity in Scotland: Progress Report: Mary-Ann Smythe (RSK-ERA Limited). (2002) (£5.00)
Summary available: Countryside and Natural Heritage Research Findings No.19

Influencing Mainstream Services: Lessons from Working for Communities Pathfinders: Alison P Brown. (2002) (£5.00)
Summary available: Development Department Research Findings No.134

"Direct What" - A Study of Direct Payments to Mental Health Service Users: Julie Ridley and Lyn Jones. (2002) (£5.00)
Summary available: Health and Community Care Research Findings No.20

Over the Threshold? An Exploration of Intensive Domiciliary Support for Older People: Lisa Curtice and Alison Petch, with Angela Hallam and Martin Knapp. (2002) (£5.00)
Summary available: Health and Community Care Research Findings No.19

Review of Care Management in Scotland: Kirsten Stalker and Isleen Campbell. (2002) (£5.00)
Summary available: Health and Community Care Research Findings No.21

Fast-Trac: Evaluation and Issues of Transferability: The Centre for Research in Lifelong Learning and The Centre for Educational Sociology. (2002) (£5.00)
Summary available: Enterprise and Lifelong Learning Research Findings No.3

Evaluation of New Deal for Young People in Scotland: Phase Two: Dorothe Bonjour, Genevieve Knight, Stephen Lissenburgh. (2002) (£5.00)
Summary available: Enterprise and Lifelong Learning Research Findings No.4

Review of Strategic Planning: Analysis of Consultation Responses: Geoff Peart Consulting. (2002) (£5.00)
Summary available: Development Department Research Findings No.136

Timber Cladding in Scotland: Ivor Davies, James Penddlebury (Highland Birchwoods) and Bruce Walker (University of Dundee). (2002) (Free)
Summary available: Countryside and Natural Heritage Research Findings No.18

Evaluation of the West Lothian Driver Improvement Scheme: Steven Hope, Dave Ingram and Becki Lancaster (NFO System Three Social Research). (2002) (£5.00)
Summary available: Development Department Research Findings No. 135

Translating, Interpreting and Communication Support Services across the Public Sector in Scotland: A Literature Review: Joanna McPake and Richard Johnstone (Scottish CILT) with Joseph Lo Bianco, Hilary McColl, Gema Rodriguez Prieto and Elizabeth Speake. (2002) (£5.00)
Summary available: Social Justice Research Findings No.6

Monitoring the National Cycling Strategy in Scotland: Scottish Cycling Development Project. (2002) (£4.00)

Climate Change: Flooding Occurrences Review: Alan Werrity, Andrew Black and Rob Duck (University of Dundee), Bill Finlinson, Neil Thurston, Simon Shackley and David Crichton (Entec UK Limited). (2002) (£5.00)
Summary available: Environment Group Research Findings No.19

Supporting Court Users: The In-Court Advice and Mediation Projects in Edinburgh Sheriff Court Research Phase 2: Elaine Samuel, Department of Social Policy University of Edinburgh. (2002) (£5.00)
Summary available: Legal Studies Research Findings No.38

Consultation on the Review of Scottish Charity Law: Paul Spicker, Sue Morris and Veronica Strachan, Centre for Public Policy and Management the Robert Gordon University. (2002) (£5.00)

Social Inclusion Research Bulletin No.7: (2002) (Free)

Equality Proofing Procedures in Drafting Legislation: International Comparisons: Fiona Mackay and Kate Bilton (Governance of Scotland Forum, University of Edinburgh). (2002) (£5.00)
Summary available: Equalities Unit Research Findings No.1

Findings from the Working for Communities: Community Involvement: Alison P Brown. (2002) (Free)
Summary only available: Development Department Research Findings No.137

Findings from the Working for Communities: The Role of a Local Co-ordinator: Alison P Brown. (2002) (Free)
Summary only available: Development Department Research Findings No.138

Racist Crime and Victimisation in Scotland: Ian Clark and Susan Moody (University of Dundee). (2002) (£5.00)
Summary available: Crime and Criminal Justice Research Findings No.58

The 2000 Scottish Crime Survey: Overview Report: MVA. (2002) (£7.00)

Domestic Violence: Findings from the 2000 Scottish Crime Survey: Suzi Macpherson. (2002) (£5.00)

Impact of Crime on Victims: Findings from the 2000 Scottish Crime Survey: Dave Ingram. (2002) (£5.00)

Drug Misuse in Scotland: Findings from the 2000 Scottish Survey: Overview Report: Fiona Fraser. (2002) (£5.00)

Violence in Scotland: Findings from the 2000 Scottish Crime Survey: MVA. (2002) (£5.00)

Young People and Crime in Scotland: Findings from the 2000 Scottish Crime Survey: MVA. (2002) (£5.00)

Housebreaking in Scotland: Findings from the 2000 Scottish Crime Survey: MVA. (2002) (£5.00)

Vehicle Crime in Scotland: Findings from the 2000 Scottish Crime Survey: MVA. (2002) (£5.00)

The 2000 Scottish Crime Survey: Analysis of the Ethnic Minority Booster Sample: Ian Clark, University of Dundee and Traci Leven, MVA. (2002) (£5.00)

Review of Research on School Travel: Derek Halden Consultancy. (2002) (£5.00)

Parole Board Decisions and Release Outcomes: Linda Hutton and Dr Liz Levy, Central Research Unit. (2002) (£5.00)

Rural Accessibility: Derek Halden (Derek Halden Consultancy), John Farrington (Aberdeen University) and Andrew Copus (Scottish Agricultural College). (2002) (£5.00)
Summary available: Development Department Research Findings No.133

The Experience of Black/Minority Ethnic Police Officers, Support Staff, Special Constables and Resigners in Scotland: Daniel Onifade (Intravires Consultants). (2002) (£5.00)

Development Department Research Programme 2002-2003: (2002) (Free)

Building Consensus for Rural Development and Planning in Scotland: A Review of Best Practice: Tim Richardson and Stephen Connelly (Department of Town and Regional Planning, University of Sheffield). (2002) (£5.00)
Summary available: Agricultural Policy Co-ordination and Rural Development Research Findings No.12

Review of Old Mineral Permissions: Alan Pollock (David Kirk & Associates). (2002) (£5.00)
Summary available: Development Department Research Findings No.140

Good Practice Guidance-Consultation with Equalities Groups: Reid-Howie Associates. (2002) (£5.00)
Central Research Unit and Equality Unit

Review of Integration among Plans for the Coast in Scotland: An Analysis of the SCF Coastal Plans Inventory: Arup Scotland and Brady Shipman Martin. (2002) (£5.00)
Summary available: Countryside and Natural Heritage Research Findings No.20

Evaluation of the Zero Tolerance "Respect" Pilot Project: Reid-Howie Associates Ltd. (2002) (£5.00)
Summary available: Crime and Criminal Justice Research Findings No.59

Managing Radioactive Waste Safely: Engaging Scotland: Deirdre Elrick, Linda Boyes and James McCormick (Scottish Council Foundation). (2002) (£5.00)
Summaries available: Environment Group Research Findings No.20 and No.21

The Review of NPPG4: Land for Mineral Working: Land Use Consultants. (2002) (£5.00)
Summary available: Development Department Research Findings No.139

Natura 2000 Scoping Study: Dr Nonie Coulthard (Logical Cobwebs Ltd). (2002) (£5.00)
Summary available: Countryside and Natural Heritage Research Findings No.21

The House Buying and Selling Process in Scotland: DTZ Pieda Consulting and NFO System Three. (2002) (£5.00)
Summary available: Development Department Research Findings No.142

Vulnerable and Intimidated Witnesses: Review of Provisions in Other Jurisdictions: Reid Howie Associates. (2002) (£5.00)
Summary available: Crime and Criminal Justice Research Findings No.60

Nature Conservation Designations and Land Value: D Roberts, D MacDonald, T Kampus, P Shannon, J Potts, F Barraclough. (2002) (£5.00)
Summary available: Countryside and Natural Heritage Research Findings No.22

National Framework for the Prevention of Suicide and Deliberate Self-Harm in Scotland: Analysis of Written Submissions to Consultation: Julie Ridley, Scottish Health Feedback. (2002) (£5.00)
Summary available: Health and Community Care Research Findings No.22

Gypsies/Travellers in Scotland: The Twice-Yearly Count – No.2. (July 2002) (Free)

Review of the Synthesis of the Environmental Impacts of Aquaculture: The Scottish Association for Marine Science and Napier University. (2002) (£5.00)

Young Carers: Assessments and Services: Pauline Banks, Eamonn Gallagher, Malcolm Hill and Sheila Riddell, Centre for the Child and Society and Strathclyde Centre for Disability Research, University of Glasgow. (2002) (£5.00)
Summary available: Health and Community Care Research Findings No.23

Domestic Abuse against Men in Scotland: David Gadd, Stephen Farrall, Damian Dallimore and Nancy Lombard, Dept of Criminology, Keele University. (2002) (£5.00)
Summary available: Crime and Criminal Justice Research Findings No.61

'Voice of the Child' Under the Children (Scotland) Act 1995: Volume 1 - Mapping Paper: K Marshall (Glasgow University), E K M Tisdall (Edinburgh University), A Cleland (Napier University). (2002) (£5.00)

'Voice of the Child' Under the Children (Scotland) Act 1995: Volume 2 - Feasibility Study: K Marshall (Glasgow University), E K M Tisdall (Edinburgh University), A Cleland (Napier University). (2002) (£5.00)
Summary available: Scotland's Children - Children (Scotland) Act 1995 Research Findings No.2

Owner Occupation Among Low Income Households in Scotland: Rebekah Widdowfield and Diana Wilkinson. (2002) (£5.00)

Monitoring and Mapping of Environmental Noise: Dr Bernadette McKell, Steve Fisher, Nigel Jones, Jane Evans and Brian Stark (Casella Stanger). (2002) (£5.00)
Summary available: Environment Group Research Findings No.23

Road Safety and Social Inclusion: Tony Graham (ODS Ltd). (2002) (£5.00)
Summary available: Development Department Research Findings No.141

Child Accidents *en route* to and from School: Colin Buchanan & Partners. (2002) (£5.00)
Summary available: Development Department Research Findings No.145

A Rural Community Gateway Website for Scotland - Scoping Study: Jenny Brogden, Joanna Gilliatt and Doug Maclean (Lambda Research and Consultancy Ltd). (2002) (£5.00)
Summary available: Agricultural Policy Co-ordination and Rural Development Research Findings No.13

City Region Boundaries Study: Derek Halden Consultancy (2002) (£5.00)
Summary available: Development Department Research Findings No.146

Why Do Parents Drive Their Children to School?: George Street Research. (2002) (£5.00)
Summary available: Development Department Research Findings No.143

Management of Work-Related Road Safety: Rebecca J Lancaster and Rachel L Ward (Entec UK Ltd). (2002) (Free)
Summary only available: Development Department Research Findings No.144

Disciplining Children: Research with Parents in Scotland: Simon Anderson and Lorraine Murray (NFO System Three); Julie Brownlie (Stirling University). (2002) (£5.00)

Results of the Scottish Staff Survey 2002: Tom Lamplugh (SE). (2002)
Summary only available: General Research Findings No.9 (Web only)

Investigations of Work Pressures within the Scottish Executive: Angela Puri (ORC International). (2002)
Summary only available: General Research Findings No.10 (Web only)

Transport Impacts of Major Health Care Developments: Faber Maunsell. (2002) (Free)
Summary only available: Development Department Research Findings No.148

Business-Related Bankruptcies Under the Bankruptcy (Scotland) Act 1985 (As Amended) - Phase 1: Scoping Study: Lambda Research and Consultancy Ltd. (2002) (£5.00)

Business Finance and Security Over Moveable Property: Jenny Hamilton, Dr Andrea Coulson and Scott Wortley (University of Strathclyde); Dave Ingram (NFO System Three). (2002) (£5.00)
Summary available: Legal Studies Research Findings No.39

Evaluation of the "Know the Score" Drugs Campaign: Doug Maclean, Joanna Gilliatt and Jenny Brogden (Lambda Research Consultancy Ltd). (2002) (£5.00)
Summary available: Crime and Criminal Justice Research Findings No.63

A Review of the First Year of the Mandatory Licensing Scheme in Houses in Multiple Occupation in Scotland: Hector Currie (School of Planning & Housing, Edinburgh College of Art/Heriot Watt University). (2002) (£5.00)
Summary available: Development Department Research Findings No.150

Social Inclusion Research Bulletin No.8: Free

Drug Treatment and Testing Orders: Evaluation of the Scottish Pilots: Susan Eley, Kathryn Gallop, Gill McIvor, Kerry Morgan, Rowdy Yates, Dept of Applied Social Science, Stirling University). (2002) (£5.00)
Summary available: Crime and Criminal Justice Research Findings No.62

Evaluation of Individual Learning Accounts - Phase 1: York Consulting Ltd. (2002) (£5.00)

Delivering Work Based Learning: Andrea Glass, Kevin Higgins and Alan McGregor, Glasgow University. (2002) (£5.00)
Summary available: Enterprise and Lifelong Learning Research Findings No.5

Education Maintenance Allowances: Evaluation of the East Ayrshire Pilot: Linda Croxford, Cathy Howieson, Christina Iannelli & Jenny Ozga. (2002) (£5.00)
Summary available: Enterprise and Lifelong Learning Research Findings No.6

Personal Injury Litigation, Negotiation and Settlement: Sam Coope and Sue Morris. (2002) (£5.00)

Enforcement of Civil Obligations in Scotland: Analysis of Consultation Reponses: Blake Stevenson Ltd. (2002) (£5.00)

Risk Assessment and Management of Serious Violent and Sexual Offenders: A Review of Current Issues: Hazel Kemshall. (2002) (£5.00)
Summary available: Crime and Criminal Justice Research Findings No.64

Serious Violent and Sexual Offenders: The Use of Risk Assessment Tools in Scotland: Gill McIvor and Hazel Kemshall. (2002) (£5.00)
Summary available: Crime and Criminal Justice Research Findings No.65

Recidivism Amongst Serious Violent and Sexual Offenders: Nancy Loucks. (2002) (£5.00)
Summary available: Crime and Criminal Justice Research Findings No.66.

The Glasgow Drug Court in Action: The First Six Months: Susan Eley, Margaret Malloch, Gill McIvor, Rowdy Yates and Alison Brown. (2002) (£5.00)

Stalking and Harassment in Scotland: Sue Morris (Robert Gordon University), Simon Anderson and Lorraine Murray (NFO System Three). (2002) (£5.00)
Summary available: Crime and Criminal Justice Research Findings No.67

Public Attitudes to the Environment in Scotland: Kerstin Hinds, Katriona Carmichael and Harvey Snowling. (2002) (Free)
Summary only available: Environment Group Research Findings No.24

Consultation on Vulnerable Adults: Analysis of Responses: Jaqueline Atkinson, Kathryn Berzins, Helen Garner (Department of Health, University of Glasgow). (2002) (£5.00)

Child Poverty in Social Inclusion Partnership: Peter A Kemp (University of York), Jo Dean and Daniel Mackay (University of Glasgow). (2002) (£5.00)

Survey of Cycling in Scotland: Tom Costley (NFO System Three). (2002) (£5.00)
Summary available: Development Department Research Findings No.149

Getting "Under the Skin" of Community Planning: Understanding Community Planning at the Community Planning Partnership Level: Robert Stevenson, RDS Consultancy Services. (2002) (£5.00)
Summary available: Local Government Research Findings No.1

Social Inclusion in Rural Areas: Innovative Projects for Young People: Emily A Bain (Social Research, Rural Research Team). (2002) (Free)
Summary only available: Land Use and Rural Policy Research Findings No.1

Review of International Best Practice in Service Delivery to Remote and Rural Areas: Frank W. Rennie, Wolfgang Greller and Mary Mackay (The Institute of Rural and Island Studies and The Scottish Centre for Information Research, Lews Castle College, UHI Millennium Institute, Stornoway). (2002) (£5.00)
Summary available: Land Use and Rural Policy Research Findings No.2

Getting Involved in Planning: Analysis of Consultation Responses: Geoff Peart Consulting. (2002) (Free)
Summary only available: Development Department Research Findings No.154/2002

Getting Involved in Planning: Perceptions of the Wider Public: Dr Paul Jenkins, Karryn Kirk, Dr Harry Smith (Centre for Environment and Human Settlements, School of Planning and Housing, Edinburgh College of Art/Heriot-Watt University). (2002) (Free)
Summary only available: Development Department Research Findings No.155/2002

Getting Involved in Planning: Summary of Evidence: Geoff Peart Consulting. (2002) (Free)
Summary only available: Development Department Research Findings No.156/2002

The Effectiveness of Tree Preservation Orders in Scotland: Roger Jessop MA (Cantab) MA (Manc) Dip TP MRTPI. (2002) (£5.00)
Summary available: Development Department Research Findings No. 151

Land Values and the Implications for Planning Policy: DTZ Pieda Consulting. (2002) (£5.00)
Summary available: Development Department Research Findings No.152

Assessment of the Effectiveness of Local Coastal Management partnerships as a Delivery Mechanism for Integrated Coastal Zone Management: ITAD Ltd, BMT Cordah Ltd. (2002) (£5.00)
Summary available: Countryside and Natural Heritage Research Findings No.23

Changing Speeding Behaviour in Scotland: An Evaluation of the 'Foolsspeed' Campaign: Martine Stead, Anne Marie MacKintosh, Stephen Tagg, Douglas Eadie (Centre for Social Marketing, University of Strathclyde, Glasgow). (2002) (£5.00)
Summary available: Development Department Research Findings No.153

Capacity Building for Community Planning: Eglinton. (2002) (£5.00)
Summary available: Local Government Research Findings No.2

How Does the Community Care? Public Attitudes to Community Care in Scotland: Lisa Curtice (Scottish Consortium for Learning Disability) and Alison Petch (Nuffield Centre for Community Care Studies). (2002) (£5.00)
Summary available: Health and Community Care Research Findings No.25

Well? What do you think? A National Scottish Survey of Public Attitudes to Mental Health, Well Being and Mental Health Problems: Richard Glendinning, Nickie Rose and Tim Buchanan with Angela Hallam. (2002) (£5.00)
Summary available: Health and Community Care Research Findings No.27

Scottish Coastal Socio-Economic Scoping Study: School of Resources, Environment and Society, University of Aberdeen. (2002) (£5.00)
Summary available: Countryside and Natural Heritage Research Findings No.24/2002

The Characteristics of People with Dementia who are Users and Non-Users of the Legal System: A Feasibility Study: Anne Mason and Heather Wilkinson. (2002) (£5.00)

Young People and Transport: MORI Scotland. (2002) (£5.00)
Summary available: Development Department Research Findings No.155

"Don't They Call It Seamless Care?" A Study of Acute Psychiatric Discharge: Lucy Simons, Alison Petch and Richard Caplan (Nuffield Centre for Community Care Studies, University of Glasgow). (2002) (£5.00)
Summary available: Health and Community Care Research Findings No.26

Research on the Private Rented Sector in Scotland: Donald Houston, Kieran Barr and Jo Dean (University of Glasgow). (2002) (£5.00)
Summary available: Development Department Research Findings No.153

Vital Voices: Helping Vulnerable Witnesses Give Evidence: Report on the Analysis of Responses to the Consultation: Elma Fitzpatrick (Consultant). (2002) (£5.00)

Community Care Research Programme: Scottish Executive Health Department Analytical Services Division. (2002) (£5.00)

Evaluation of the Scottish Prison Service's Tendering Process for Social Work Contracts: Tony Homer; (Craigforth Consulting). (2002) (£5.00)

Her Majesty's Inspectorate of Prisons: Scope and Focus: Reid Howie Associates Ltd. (2002) (£5.00)

The Status of Traditional Scottish Animal Breeds and Plant Varieties and the Implications for Biodiversity: I.A. Wright and A.J.I Dalziel (MacAuley Institute) and R P Ellis (Scottish Crop Research Institute). (2003) (£5.00)
Summary available: Countryside and Natural Heritage Research Findings No.25

Seat Belt Wearing in Scotland: A Second Study on Compliance: Archie Burns, Mark Kummerer and Neil C Macdonald (Halcrow Group Limited). (2003) (£5.00)
Summary available: Development Department Research Findings No.157

Standards of Care and Regulation of Care Services in Scotland: Charlotte Pearson and Sheila Riddell (Strathclyde Centre for Disability Research). (2003) (£5.00)
Summary available: Health and Community Care Research Findings No.24

Crime and Criminal Justice Research Agenda Criminal Justice Research Branch. (2003) (£5.00)

Mortgage Arrears and Repossessions in Scotland: Emma McCallum and Ewan McCaig (MVA). (2003) (£5.00)
Summary available: Development Department Research Findings No.158

Consultation on a Physical Activity Strategy for Scotland: Analysis of Responses: Sheila Henderson; (Reid-Howie Associates). (2003) (£5.00)
Summary available: Health and Community Care Research Findings No.28

Liquor Licensing and Public Disorder : Review of Literature and Other Controls/Audit of Local Initiative: Reid Howie Associates Ltd. (2003) (£5.00)
Summary available: Crime and Criminal Justice Research Findings No.68

Omnibus Survey: Testing Public Opinion on Licensing Laws and Alcohol Consumption: Deena Kara and Linda Hutton (Scottish Opinion Ltd). (2003) (£2.00)

Underage Drinking and the Illegal Purchase of Alcohol: Paul Bradshaw. (2003) (£2.00)

Asylum Seekers in Scotland: Aileen Barclay, Alison Bowed, Iain Ferguson, Duncan Sim and Maggie Valenti; with assistance from Soraya Fard and Sherry MacIntosh; (University of Stirling). (2003) (£5.00)
Summary available: Social Justice Research Findings No.2

Evaluation of the Drug Driving TV Advert: Rachel Ormston; NFO Social Research. (2003) (£5.00)
Summary available: Development Department Research Findings No.159

New Directions for Land Management Schemes in Scotland's National Parks: Land Use Consultants, Glasgow. (2003) (£5.00)
Summary available: Countryside and Natural Heritage Research Findings No.26

Social Inclusion Bulletin No.9: Social Inclusion Research Branch (Ruth Bryan). (2003) (Free)

Determined Differences: Rent Structures in Scottish Social Housing: Alison More, Jeanette Findlay, Kenneth Gibb, Diana Kasparova and Carl Mills (Department of Urban Studies, University of Glasgow). (2003) (£5.00)
Summary available: Development Department Research Findings No.161/2003

Tracking Homelessness: A Feasibility Study: Kevin Pickering, Suzanne Fitzpatrick, Kerstin Hinds, Peter Lynn and Sarah Tipping. (2003) (Web only)
Summary available: Development Department Research Findings No.162/2003

Sexual Orientation Research Phase 1: A Review of Methodological Approaches: Sally McManus (National Centre for Social Research). (2003) (£5.00)

Sexual Orientation Research Phase 2: The Future of LGBT Research – Perspectives of Community Organisations: Carl McLean and William O'Connor (National Centre for Social Research). (2003) (£5.00)
Summary available: Social Justice Research Findings No.3/2003

Modern Title and Condition Deeds in Scotland and their Effectiveness in Securing Common Repairs: Ann Flint, James Barrowman and Derek O'Carroll (Ann Flint & Associates). (2003) (£5.00)
Summary available: Development Department Research Findings No.160/2003

Impact of Childcare Support for Lone Parent Students: Fiona Ballantyne, Claire Hendry and Ralph Leishman (4-consulting Ltd). (2003) (£5.00)
Summary available: Social Justice Research Findings No.1/2003

Minority and Social Diversity in Legal Education: Simon Anderson, Lorraine Murray (NFO System Three) and Paul Maharg (University of Strathclyde). (2003) (£5.00)

Direct Supply of Medicines in Scotland: Evaluation of a Pilot Scheme: Ellen Schafheutle and Peter Noyce (University of Manchester), Christine Sheehy and Lyn Jones (Scottish Health Feedback). (2003) (Free)
Summary only available: Health and Community Care Research Findings No.29

Direct Supply of Medicines in Scotland: Extended Monitoring of a Pilot Scheme: Christine Sheehy and Lyn Jones (Scottish Health Feedback). (2003) (Free)
Summary only available: Health and Community Care Research Findings No.30

Evaluation of the Working for Communities Programme: DTZ Pieda Consulting. (2003) (£5.00)
Summary available: Development Department Research Findings No.163/2003

Bus Passenger Satisfaction Survey: Colin Buchanan & Partners. (2003) (Free)
Summary only available: Development Department Research Findings No.164/2003

Scoping Study of Older People in Rural Scotland: Dr Lorna Philip, Dr Natasha Mauthner, Dr Euan Phimister (University of Aberdeen) and Dr Alana Gilbert (Macaulay Institute). (2003) (£5.00)
Summary available: Land Use and Rural Policy Research Findings No.3/2003

Consultation Paper on the Mental Health Law Research Programme. (2003) (£5.00)

Public Attitudes to Access to the Countryside: NFO System Three. (2003) (£5.00)
Summary available: Countryside and Natural Heritage Research Findings No.27/2003

Development Department Research Programme 2003-2004. (2003) (Free)

Results of the Scottish Executive Staff Survey: Tom Lamplugh. (2003) (Free)
Summary only available: General Research Findings No.11

Evaluation of National Planning Policy Guideline 15 (NPPG15): Rural Development: Land Use Consultants. (2003) (£5.00)
Summary available: Development Department Research Findings No.165/2003

Management Needs Resource Analysis: A Report to the Best Value Task Force: Gillian Lancaster and Iain MacAllister. (2003) (£5.00)

The Witness Service Five Years On: An Evaluation in 2003: David Lobley and David Smith (Lancaster University). (2003) (£5.00)
Summary available: Crime and Criminal Justice Research Findings No.72/2003

Scottish Compact Baseline Review: Keith Hayton (Gen Consulting). (2003) (£5.00)
Summary available: Social Justice Research Findings No.5/2003

The Fife Drug Court in Action: The First Six Months: Margaret Malloch, Susan Eley, Gill McIvor, Kathlene Beaton and Rowdy Yates (Department of Applied Social Science, University of Stirling). (2003) (£5.00)
Summary available: Crime and Criminal Justice Research Findings No.69/2003

The Glasgow Drug Court in Action: The First Six Months: Susan Eley, Margaret Malloch, Gill McIvor, Rowdy Yates and Alison Brown. (2003) (Free)
Summary only available: Crime and Criminal Justice Research Findings No.70/2003

Establishing Drug Courts in Scotland: Early Experiences of the Pilot Drug Courts in Glasgow and Fife: Gill McIvor, Susan Eley, Margaret Malloch and Rowdy Yates. (2003) (Free)
Summary only available: Crime and Criminal Justice Research Findings No.71/2003

External-to-Vehicle Driver Distraction: Dr Brendan Wallace (HFAL). (2003) (£5.00)
Summary available: Development Department Research Findings No.168/2003

Living in Scotland: An Urban-Rural Analysis of the Scottish Household Survey: Scottish Executive Environment and Rural Development Department, Social Research Branch with assistance from Scottish Agricultural College. (2003) (Web only)
Summary available: Land Use and Rural Policy Research Findings No.4/2003 (Web only)

Gypsies/Travellers in Scotland: The Twice-Yearly Count – No.3 (January 2003) (Free)

The Speeding Driver: Who, How and Why?: S G Stradling and M Campbell (Transport Research Institute, Napier University), I A Allan, R S J Gorell, J P Hill and M G Winter (TRL Ltd) and S Hope (NFO System Three Social Research). (2003) (£5.00)
Summary available: Development Department Research Findings No.170/2003

Evaluation of Bikesafe Scotland: Rachel Ormston, Anna Dudleston, Stephen Pearson (NFO Social Research) and Steve Stradling (Napier University). (2003) (£5.00)
Summary available: Development Department Research Findings No.169/2003

Public Attitudes to Windfarms: Simon Braunholtz (MORI Scotland). (2003) (£5.00)
Summary available: General Research Findings No.12/2003

Deposit Guarantee Schemes in Scotland: Julie Rugg (Centre for Housing Policy, University of York). (2003) (£5.00)
Summary available: Development Department Research Findings No.166/2003

Social Inclusion Bulletin No.10: (2003) (Free)

Life in Low Income Families in Scotland: Research Report: John H McKendrick, Sarah Cunningham-Burley and Kathryn Backett-Milburn (Centre for Research on Families and Relationships (CRFR), University of Edinburgh). (2003) (£5.00)
Summary available: Social Justice Research Findings No.6/2003

Life in Low Income Families in Scotland: A Review of the Literature: John H McKendrick, Sarah Cunningham-Burley and Kathryn Backett-Milburn (Centre for Research on Families and Relationships (CRFR), University of Edinburgh). (2003) (£5.00)
Summary available: Social Justice Research Findings No.6/2003

Evaluation of the National Care Standards Consultations: Ruth Whatling (Civic Participation and Consultation Research Team, Scottish Executive). (2003) (£5.00)
Summary available: Health and Community Care Research Findings No.31/2003

Good Practice in Rural Development No 8: Innovative Methods of Service Delivery in Rural Scotland: A Good Practice Guide: Jon Pickering (Centre for Advanced Studies, University of Cardiff). (2003) (£5.00)

Review of Scottish Executive Road Safety Research Campaign 1998-2003: Janet Ruiz (Transport and Planning Research Branch). (2003) (£5.00)

Evaluation of the Children's Traffic Club in Scotland: New Nursery and Playgroup Pack: Tony Graham, Katy Fyfe, Mark Hughes and Anne Murray (ODS Ltd). (2003) (£5.00)
Summary available: Development Department Research Findings No.172/2003

The Role of Mediation in Tackling Neighbour Disputes and Anti-Social Behaviour: Alison P Brown, Aileen Barclay, Richard Simmons and Susan Eley (Dept of Applied Social Science, Stirling University). (2003) (£5.00)
Summary available: Development Department Research Findings No.167/2003

Legal Studies Research Agenda: (2003) (Free)

Barriers to Modal Shift: Derek Halden Consultancy. (2003) (£5.00)
Summary available: Development Department Research Findings No.171/2003

Mental Health Officer Services: Structures and Support: Allyson McCollam, Joanne McLean, Jean Gordon and Kristina Moodie (Scottish Development Centre for Mental Health). (2003) (£5.00)
Summary available: Health and Community Care Research Findings No.32/2003

Omnibus Survey of Small Businesses in Scotland: Databuild. (2003) (£5.00)
Summary available: Enterprise and Lifelong Learning Research Findings No.7/2003

Options for Change: Research on the Content of a Possible Planning Bill: Jeremy Rowan Robinson. (2003) (Free)

Attitudes to Discrimination in Scotland: Catherine Bromley and John Curtice (NatCen Scotland). (2003) (£5.00)
Summary available: Social Justice Research Findings No.7/2003

Youth Transitions: Patterns of Vulnerability and Processes of Social Inclusion: Andy Furlong, Fred Cartmel (Department of Sociology & Anthropology, University of Glasgow), Andy Biggart (School of Policy Studies, University of Ulster at Coleraine), Helen Sweeting and Patrick West (MRC Social and Public Health Sciences Unit). (2003) (£5.00)
Summary available: Enterprise and Lifelong Learning Research Findings No.8/2003

Legal Information and Advice Provision in Scotland: A Review of Evidence: Blake Stevenson Ltd with Office of Public Management. (2003) (Web only)
Summary available: Legal Studies Research Findings No.40/2003

Diversity in the Public Appointments Process in Scotland: Reid Howie Associates Ltd. (2003) (£5.00)
Summary available: Social Justice Research Findings No.8/2003

Part-Time Firefighters: Sue Granville (George Street Research Limited). (2003) (£5.00)
Summary available: General Research Findings No.13/2003

Focus Groups with Minority Ethnic Communities: Blake Stevenson Ltd. (2003) (Web only)

Evaluating Family Health Nursing Through Education and Practice: Colin Macduff and Dr Bernice J M West. (2003) (£5.00)
Summary available: Health and Community Care Research Findings No.33/2003

An Evaluation of the Protection from Abuse (Scotland) Act 2001: Dr Kate Cavanagh, Clare Connelly (University of Glasgow) and Jane Scoular (University of Strathclyde). (2003) (£5.00)
Summary available: Legal Studies Research Findings No.41/2003

National Survey of Local Government Candidates, 2003: Iain MacAllister. (2003) (£5.00)

Safely to School: A Study of Safer Routes to School in the Classroom: Valerie Wilson, Kevin Lowden, John Hall (The SCRE Centre), Tony Graham and Katy Fyfe (ODS Ltd). (2003) (£5.00)
Summary available: Development Department Research Findings No.173/2003

Children's Attitudes to Sustainable Transport: Derek Halden Consultancy. (2003) (Web only)
Summary available: Development Department Research Findings No.174/2003

Evaluation of the Domestic Abuse Service Development Fund 2000-2002: Reid Howie Associates Ltd. (2003) (£5.00)
Summary available: Crime and Criminal Justice Research Findings No.73/2003

Victims of Volume Crime in Scotland: Perceptions of the Police and the Criminal Justice System: Brian Williams, Gill McIvor, Mike Semenchuk, Maggie Valenti, Roy Bailey, Alison Brown and Margaret Malloch (De Montfort University and University of Stirling). (2004) (£5.00)
Summary available: Crime and Criminal Justice Research Findings No.74/2004

The Evaluation of the Scottish Rural Partnership Fund: Larch Research Ltd & Associates. (2004) (Web Only)
Summary only available: Land Use and Rural Policy Research Findings No.5/2004

Mental Health Law Research Programme: Analysis of Responses to Consultation: Rosemary Rushmer and Angela Hallam. (2004) (£5.00)

Analysis of Responses to "Review of Historic Scotland": Linda Nicholson and Sue Granville (George Street Research Limited). (2004) (£5.00)
Summary available: General Research Findings No.14/2004

The Effectiveness of NPPG8: Town Centres & Retailing: CB Richard Ellis (University of Stirling, Institute for Retail Studies) and Colin Buchanan and Partners. (2004) (Free)
Summary only available: Development Department Research Findings No.175/2004

Review of the Code of Practice for Part 5 of the Adults with Incapacity (Scotland) Act 2000 and Related Issues: Analysis of Written Submissions to Consultation: Hannah Drinkwater, Heather Wilkinson, Fran Wasoff, Anne Mason and Shirley Davidson. (2004) (£5.00)
Summary available: Health and Community Care Research Findings No.34/2004

Involving Older People: Lessons for Community Planning: Belinda Dewar, Chris Jones and Fiona O'May (Scottish Centre for the Promotion of the Older Person's Agenda, Queen Margaret University College). (2004) (Web only)
Summary available: Social Justice Research Findings No.9/2004

The Operation and Effectiveness of National Planning Policy Guideline (NPPG) 16: Opencast Coal and Related Minerals: Alan Pollock (DKA Planning). (2004) (£5.00)
Summary available: Development Department Research Findings No.176/2004

Gypsies/Travellers in Scotland: The Twice-Yearly Count – No.4: July 2003: Research Consultancy Services. (2004) (Free)

Working for Families: Lessons from the Pilot Projects (Stage 1): Keith Hayton and Michelle Myron (GEN Consulting). (2004) (£5.00)
Summary available: Social Justice Research Findings No.11/2004 (Web only)

Preventing Domestic Abuse in the Western Isles: The Community Perspective: Morag MacNeil, Bob Stradling, Catherine Ann MacNeill, Ann Bethune and Brian MacDonald. (2004) (Free)
Summary only available: Crime and Criminal Justice Research Findings No.75/2004

Evaluation of the Scottish Domestic Abuse Helpline: Louise Brown Research. (2004) (£5.00)
Summary available: Crime and Criminal Justice Research Findings No.76/2004

Attitudes to Car Use and Modal Shift in Scotland: Simon Anderson and Stephen G Stradling (National Centre for Social Research (NatCen) Scotland and Transport Research Institute, Napier University). (2004) (£5.00)

The Consultation on Civil Partnership Registration: Analysis of the Responses: Veronica Strachan, Paul Spicker, Sue Morris and Tatiana Damjanovic (Centre for Public Policy and Management, The Robert Gordon University). (2004) (£5.00)

A Preliminary Analysis of the Bail/Custody Decision in Relation to Female Accused: Kevin Brown, Peter Duff and Fiona Leverick (Aberdeen University, School of Law). (2004) (£5.00)

Offending on Bail: An Analysis of the Use and Impact of Aggravated Sentences for Bail Offenders: Kevin Brown, Fiona Leverick and Peter Duff. (2004) (£5.00)

Scottish Child Contact Centres: Characteristics of Centre Users and Centre Staff: Louyse McConnell-Trevillion and Samantha Coope with Emily Postan and Louise Lane (Scottish Executive Legal Studies Research Team). (2004) (£5.00)
Summary available: Legal Studies Research Findings No.42/2004

Building Bridges? Expectations and Experiences of Child Contact Centres in Scotland: Kerry Sproston, Kandy Woodfield with Kay Tisdall (National Centre for Social Research (Scotland) and Children in Scotland/University of Edinburgh). (2004) (£5.00)

Family Formation and Dissolution: Trends and Attitudes Among the Scottish Population: Anita Morrison, Debbie Headrick (Legal Studies Research Team, Scottish Executive), Fran Wasoff and Sarah Morton (Centre for Research on Families and Relationships, University of Edinburgh). (2004) (Free)
Summary only available: Legal Studies Research Findings No.43/2004

The Nicholson Committee Report on Liquor Licensing Laws in Scotland: Analysis of Consultation Responses: Anna Dudleston and Lorraine Murray (TNS Social Research). (2004) (£5.00)

Modern Apprenticeships: Improving Completion Rates: Jim Gallacher, Susan Whittaker, Beth Crossan (Centre for Research in Lifelong Learning, Glasgow Caledonian University) and Vince Mills (Scottish Centre for Work-Based Learning, Glasgow Caledonian University). (2004) (£5.00)
Summary available: Enterprise and Lifelong Learning Research Findings No.9/2004

Social Inclusion Research Bulletin No.11: (2004) (Free)

Refugee and Asylum Seekers in Scotland: A Skills and Aspirations Audit: Leyla Charlaff, Kushtrim Ibrani, Michelle Lowe, Ruth Marsden and Laura Turney (Scottish Executive and Scottish Refugee Council). (2004) (£5.00)
Summary available: Social Justice Research Findings No.10/2004

Bathing Water Use in Scotland: TNS Travel and Tourism. (2004) (£5.00)
Summary available: Office of Chief Researcher Research Findings No.3/2004 (Web only)

Credit Union Training and Skills Audit: Michael Chapman, Anne Boyle, Francoise Rutherford and Fiona Wager (Centre for Research into Socially Inclusive Services (CRSIS), Heriot-Watt University, Edinburgh). (2004) (£5.00)
Summary available: Social Justice Research Findings No.12/2004 (Web only)

Academy Bulletin No.1/2004: Scottish Academy for Health Policy and Management Position Paper - March 2004. (2004) (Free)

Evaluation of People's Panels and People's Juries in Social Inclusion Partnerships: Robert Stevenson (RDS Consulting) in association with Peter Gibson (Craigforth) and Clare Lardner (Clarity). (2004) (£5.00)
Summary available: Development Department Research Findings No.177/2004

Early Approaches to Monitoring and Evaluation of the Better Neighbourhood Services Fund: Liz Shiel and Ian Clark (DTZ Pieda Consulting). (2004) (£5.00)

Developing Local Outcome Agreement for the Better Neighbourhood Services Fund: Liz Shiel and Ian Clark (DTZ Pieda Consulting). (2004) (£5.00)

Older People and Community in Scotland: A Review of Recent Research: Charlotte MacDonald. (2004) (£5.00)
Summary available: Health and Community Care Research Findings No.35/2004

The Scottish Human Rights Commission: Analysis of Consultation Responses: Fiona MacDonald and Ed Thomson. (2004) (£5.00)

Review of the Early Implementation of the Resource Use Measure: Craigforth Consultants. (2004) (£5.00)
Summary available: Health and Community Care Research Findings No.36/2004

Community Legal Service: Assessing Needs for Legal Advice in Scotland: Overview Report: James Law, Sinead Assenti, Gareth Barton, Kirsty McKissock (Market Research UK Ltd); Professor Deborah Baker, Steve Barrow (University of Salford); and Dan Cookson (SeeIT Ltd). (2004) (£5.00)
Summary available: Legal Studies Research Findings No.44/2004

Assessing Need for Legal Advice in Argyll & Bute: James Law, Sinead Assenti, Gareth Barton, Kirsty McKissock (Market Research UK Ltd); Professor Deborah Baker, Steve Barrow (University of Salford); Dan Cookson (SeeIT Ltd); and Catherine Palmer (Scottish Executive). (2004) (Free)
Summary only available: Legal Studies Research Findings No.45/2004

Assessing Need for Legal Advice in Edinburgh: James Law, Sinead Assenti, Gareth Barton, Kirsty McKissock (Market Research UK Ltd); Professor Deborah Baker, Steve Barrow (University of Salford); Dan Cookson (SeeIT Ltd); and Catherine Palmer (Scottish Executive). (2004) (Free)
Summary only available: Legal Studies Research Findings No.46/2004

Assessing Need for Legal Advice in Fife: James Law, Sinead Assenti, Gareth Barton, Kirsty McKissock (Market Research UK Ltd); Professor Deborah Baker, Steve Barrow (University of Salford); Dan Cookson (SeeIT Ltd); and Catherine Palmer (Scottish Executive). (2004) (Free)
Summary only available: Legal Studies Research Findings No.47/2004

Assessing Need for Legal Advice in Glasgow West: James Law, Sinead Assenti, Gareth Barton, Kirsty McKissock (Market Research UK Ltd); Professor Deborah Baker, Steve Barrow (University of Salford); Dan Cookson (SeeIT Ltd); and Catherine Palmer (Scottish Executive). (2004) (Free)
Summary only available: Legal Studies Research Findings No.48/2004

Community Legal Service: Assessing Needs for Legal Advice in Scotland: Technical & Geographic Report: James Law, Sinead Assenti, Gareth Barton, Kirsty McKissock (Market Research UK Ltd); Professor Deborah Baker, Steve Barrow (University of Salford); and Dan Cookson (SeeIT Ltd). (2004) (Web only)

Older People in Scotland: Results from the Scottish Household Survey 1999-2002: Charlotte MacDonald and Gillian Raab (Napier University). (2004) (£5.00)
Summary available: Health and Community Care Research Findings No.37/2004

On the Borderline? People with Learning Disabilities and/or Autistic Spectrum Disorders in Secure, Forensic and other Specialist Settings: Fiona Myers (Scottish Development Centre for Mental Health). (2004) (£5.00)
Summary available: Health and Community Care Research Findings No.39/2004

Monitoring Free Local Off-Peak Bus Travel for Older and Disabled People: Colin Buchanan and Partners. (2004) (£5.00)
Summary available: Development Department Research Findings No.179/2004

Monitoring Free Local Off-Peak Bus Travel for Older and Disabled People:
Technical Report 1: Passenger Generation Surveys
Technical Report 2: Bus Occupancy Surveys
Technical Report 3: User Surveys
Technical Report 4: Bus Boarding Data
Technical Report 5: Demographic Model
Colin Buchanan and Partners. (2004) (Web only)

Bus Passenger Satisfaction Survey 2003: Colin Buchanan and Partners. (2004) (£5.00)
Summary available: Development Department Research Findings No.178/2004

Model Policies in the Land Use Planning in Scotland: A Scoping Study: MG Lloyd and DM Peel (The Geddes Institute, University of Dundee). (2004) (£5.00)
Summary available: Development Department Research Findings No.182/2004

Scotland's International Image: Communications and Strategic Research Team. (2004) (Free)
Summary only available: Office of Chief Researcher Research Findings No.4/2004

Higher Education Review Phase 3: Evaluation of the Review Process: Jenny Stewart and Jo Fawcett (George Street Research Ltd). (2004) (£5.00)

Evaluation of Revised Planning Controls over Telecommunication Development: MG Lloyd, DM Peel and PW Roberts (The Geddes Institute, University of Dundee) and J Riley (Addleshaw Booth). (2004) (£5.00)
Summary available Development Department Research Findings No.183/2004

Black and Minority Ethnic Communities and Homelessness in Scotland: Gina Netto, Cathy Fancy, Hal Pawson, Delia Lomax, Satnam Sing and Sinead Powers. (2004) (£5.00)
Summary available: Development Department Research Findings No.184/2004

Gypsies/Travellers in Scotland The Twice Yearly Count – No 5: January 2004: Research Consultancy Service. (2004) (Free)

The Hamilton Sheriff Youth Court Pilot: The First Six Months: Gill McIvor, Alison Brown, Susan Eley, Margaret Malloch, Cathy Murray, Laura Piacentini and Reece Walters. (2004) (£5.00)
Summary available: Crime and Criminal Justice Research Findings No.77/2004

Transport Provision for Disabled People in Scotland: Progress Since 1998: Reid Howie Associates Ltd. (2004) (£5.00)
Summary available: Development Department Research Findings No.180/2004

An Evaluation of the Community Legal Service Pilot Partnerships: Sarah Bulloch (Legal Studies Research Team, Scottish Executive). (2004) (Free)
Summary only available: Legal Studies Research Findings No.49/2004

Planning and Community Involvement in Scotland: PPS Local and Regional Ltd. (2004) (£5.00)
Summary available: Development Department Research Findings No.185/2004

The Elusive Nature of the Learning Society: A Profile of Adult Participation in Education and Training in Scotland: Prof Maria Slowey (Dept of Adult and Continuing Education, University of Glasgow). (2004) (£5.00)
Summary available: Enterprise and Lifelong Learning Research Findings No.11/2004

Modernising NHS Dental Services in Scotland: Analysis of the Consultation Responses: Linda Nicholson (The Research Shop). (2004) (£5.00)
Summary available: Office of Chief Researcher Research Findings No.5/2004

Assessing the Impact of the Central Heating Programme on Tackling Fuel Poverty: Survey of Households included in 2001-2002: Bill Sheldrick and David Hepburn (Alembic Research). (2004) (Free) (Web only)
Summary available: Development Department Research Findings No.187/2004

Review of Green Belt Policy in Scotland: Glen Bramley, Cliff Hague, Karryn Kirk, Alan Prior, Jeremy Raemakers and Harry Smith (School of the Built Environment, Heriot-Watt University) and Andrew Robinson and Rosie Bushnell (Robinson Association). (2004) (£5.00)
Summary available: Development Department Research Findings No.188/2004

Green Jobs Strategy Review: Optimat Ltd. (2004) (Free) (Web only)

Research Literature Review on Prescribing: Jane Harris, Julie Taylor (School of Nursing and Midwifery, University of Dundee) and Clare Mackie (School of Pharmacy, University of Kent). (2004) (£5.00)
Summary available: Health and Community Care Research Findings No.40/2004

Review of the Rural Petrol Stations Grant Scheme: Steer Davies Gleave. (2004) (Free) (Web Only)
Summary available: Development Department Research Findings No.186/2004

The Use of Mediation to Settle Civil Justice Disputes: A Review of Evidence: Fiona M MacDonald (Legal Studies Research Team, Scottish Executive). (2004) (Free)
Summary only available: Legal Studies Research Findings No.50/2004

Lead Tenancy Schemes in Scotland: Julie Rugg and David Rhodes (Centre for Housing Policy, University of York). (2004) (£5.00)
Summary available: Development Department Research Findings No.189/2004

Sector Skills Alliance Scotland: Customer Satisfaction Survey and Evaluation 2003-2004: Blake Stevenson Ltd. (2004) (Web Only)
Summary available: Enterprise and Lifelong Learning Research Findings No.12/2004 (Web Only)

The Provision of Advice about Housing to Prisoners in Scotland: An Evaluation of the Projects Funded by the Rough Sleepers Initiative: Reid-Howie Associates Ltd. (2004) (£5.00)
Summary available: Development Department Research Findings No.181/2004

Historic Scotland Stakeholder Research: Robert Stevenson (RDS Consulting). (2004) (£5.00)
Summary available: Office of Chief Researcher Research Findings No.6/2004 (Web only)

Social Inclusion Research Bulletin No.12/2004: (2004) (Free)

Fathers as Co-Parents: How Non-Resident Fathers Construe Family Situations: Graeme B Wilson, John B Gillies and Gillian M Mayes (Department of Psychology, University of Glasgow). (2004) (Free)
Summary only available: Legal Studies Research Findings No.52/2004

Evaluation of the Scottish Skills Fund: John Rodger and Alison Hunter (York Consulting Ltd). (2004) (Web only).
Summary available: Enterprise and Lifelong Learning Research Findings No.13/2004 (Web only)

Evaluation of the 2003/2004 Festive Drink Drive Campaign: mruk Ltd. (2004) (Web only).
Summary available: Development Department Research Findings No.191/2004

Contact Applications Involving Allegations of Domestic Abuse: Feasibility Study: Ann McGuckin and Brian McGuckin (AMA Consultancy). (2004) (Web only).
Summary available: Legal Studies Research Findings No.51/2004

The Interaction Between Land Use Planning and Environmental Regulation: Environmental Resources Management Ltd. (2004) (£5.00)
Summary available: Development Department Research Findings No.192/2004

Management of School/College Partnerships and the Main Operational Issues Involved: Linzie Wood (Enterprise, Transport and Lifelong Learning Department, Scottish Executive). (2004) (Web only)
Summary available: Enterprise and Lifelong Learning Research Findings No.14/2004 (Web only)

Collaboration Between Schools and Further Education Colleges in Scotland: Literature Review: Anne Galloway (Enterprise, Transport and Lifelong Learning Department, Scottish Executive). (2004) (Web only)
Summary available: Enterprise and Lifelong Learning Research Findings No.15/2004 (Web only)

School Pupils' Attitudes to Further Education: Carole Millar Research. (2004) (Web only)
Summary available: Enterprise and Lifelong Learning Research Findings No.16/2004 (Web only)

Family Law Consultation: Interactive Focus Group Exercise: mruk research Ltd. (2004) (£5.00)

Improving Family Law in Scotland: Analysis of Written Consultation Responses: Linda Nicholson (The Research Shop). (2004) (£5.00)

Suicide and Suicidal Behaviour: Establishing the Territory for a Series of Research Reviews: Joanne McLean, Amy Woodhouse (Scottish Development Centre for Mental Health) and Stephen Platt (Research Unit in Health, Behaviour and Change, University of Edinburgh). (2004) (£5.00)
Summary available: Health and Community Care Research Findings No.42/2004

Private Retirement Housing and the Title Conditions (Scotland) Act 2003: Malcolm J Fisk and Sandra Prida (Insight Social Research Ltd). (2004) (Web only)
Summary available: Development Department Research Findings No.193/2004

Modernising NHS Community Pharmacy in Scotland: Analysis of Consultation Responses: Linda Nicholson (The Research Shop). (2004) (£5.00)
Summary available: Health Department Research Findings No.1/2004

Academy Bulletin No.2/2004: Scottish Academy for Health Policy and Management: Bulletin: September 2004. (2004) (Free)

Parental Attitudes to Road Safety Education: ODS Ltd with Market Research UK Ltd. (2004) (£5.00)
Summary available: Development Department Research Findings No.190/2004

Motorcycle Accidents and Casualties in Scotland 1992-2002: Barry Sexton, John Fletcher and Kevin Hamilton (TRL Ltd). (2004) (£5.00)
Summary available: Development Department Research Findings No.194/2004

Reconviction Following Drug Treatment and Testing Orders: Gill McIvor (Social Work Research Centre, Dept of Applied Social Science, University of Stirling). (2004) (£5.00)

The Adults with Incapacity (Scotland) Act 2000: Learning from Experience: Jan Killeen (Alzheimer Scotland – Action on Dementia) and Fiona Myers (Scottish Development Centre for Mental Health) with Allison Brisbane, Kirsty Coulson, Kate Fearnley, Jean Gordon, Dorothy Keith, Joanne Maclean, Maureen Thom and Amy Woodhouse. (2004) (£5.00)
Summary available: Legal Studies Research Findings No.53/2004

Research Review on Tackling Delayed Discharge: Scottish School of Primary Care (Gill Hubbard (University of Glasgow), Guro Huby (University of Edinburgh), Sally Wyke (Scottish School of Primary Care) and Markus Themessl-Huber (University of Dundee)). (2004) (Web only)
Summary available: Health and Community Care Research Findings No.41/2004

The Use of Human Rights Legislation in the Scottish Courts: Paul Greenhill, Tom Mullen, and Jim Murdoch (Glasgow University), Sarah Craig (Stirling University), Alan Miller (Strathclyde University). (2004) (£5.00)
Summary available: Legal Studies Research Findings No.54/2004

Finance and Central Services Department Research Programme 2004-2005: (2004) (Web only)

An Evaluation of Appropriate Adult Schemes in Scotland: Dr Lindsay Thomson, Viki Galt, Dr Rajan Darjee (Division of Psychiatry, University of Edinburgh) (2004) (Free)
Summary only available: Crime and Criminal Justice Research Findings No.78/2004

The Draft Charities and Trustee Investment (Scotland) Bill: Focus Group Discussions with the General Public: Todd Associates/Van Döet Consulting. (2004) (Web only)
Summary available: Social Justice Research Findings No.14/2004 (Web only)

Staff Survey Findings 2004: (2004) (Web only)
Summary only available: Office of Chief Researcher Research Findings No.7/2004

The Licensing (Scotland) Bill: An Analysis of Consultation Responses: Fiona M MacDonald (Scottish Executive). (2004) (£5.00)

Integrated Ticketing in Scotland: Needs Analysis and Options: Rachel Ormston (TNS Social Research), Kevin Hamilton, Claire Vance, Iain York, Paul Emerson (TRL), James Cooper, Tom Rye, Steve Stradling (TRi, Napier University). (2004) (Web only)
Summary available: Development Department Research Findings No.195/2004

Public Attitudes to the National Health Service in Scotland – 2004 Survey: Nickie Rose and Richard Glendinning (NOP Social and Political) with Roy Carr-Hill (University of York). (2004) (£5:00)
Summary available: Health and Community Care Research Findings No.43/2004

Gypsies/Travellers in Scotland: The Twice-Yearly Count – No.6: July 2004: Research Consultancy Services. (2004) (Free)

Scottish Executive Stakeholder Survey 2004: Office of Chief Researcher. (2004) (Web only)
Summary only available: Office of Chief Researcher Research Bulletin No.1/2004

Recruitment and Retention Issues in Better Neighbourhood Services Fund Programmes: Liz Shiel and Ian Clark (Tribal HCH). (2004) (Web only)

Scottish Crime Survey 2003: Susan McVie, Siobhan Campbell and Korin Lebov. (2004) (£5:00)

Initial Review of the Implementation of Business Learning Accounts Pilot: Cambridge Policy Consultants Ltd. (2004) (Web only)
Summary available: Enterprise and Lifelong Learning Research Findings No.17/2004 (Web only)

Well? What do you think? (2004): The Second National Scottish Survey of Public Attitudes to Mental Health, Mental Well-Being and Mental Health Problems: Simon Braunholtz, Sara Davidson and Susan King (MORI Scotland). (2004) (£5.00)
Summary available: Health and Community Care Research Findings No.44/2004

Disability and Employment in Scotland: A Review of the Evidence Base: Sheila Riddell and Theresa Tinklin (University of Edinburgh), Pauline Banks (University of Glasgow). (2005) (£5.00)
Summary available: Social Justice Research Findings No.15/2005

National "English for Speakers of Other Languages" (ESOL) Strategy: Mapping Exercise and Scoping Study: Catherine Rice, Neil McGregor, Hilary Thomson and Hiro Udagawa (University of Abertay Dundee). (2005) (Web only)
Summary available: Enterprise and Lifelong Learning Research Findings No.19/2005 (Web only)

Religious Discrimination and Sectarianism in Scotland: A Brief Review of Evidence (2002–2004): Louise McAspurren (Development Department, Analytical Services Division). (2005) (Web only)

Scottish Business Attitudes to Research, Development and Innovation: DTZ Pieda Consulting. (2005) (Web only)
Summary only available: Enterprise and Lifelong Learning Research Findings No.20/2005

Public Attitudes to the Environment in Scotland. (2005) (Web only)

Public Attitudes to the Environment in Scotland – Technical Report: Mike Barber and Andra Laird (George Street Research), Gillian Rabb. (2005) (Web only)

Enhancing Sexual Wellbeing in Scotland – A Sexual Health and Relationship Strategy: Analysis of Written Responses to the Public Consultation: Anna Dudleston, Lorraine Murray, Rachel Ormiston and Judith Harkins (TNS Social). (2005) (£5.00)
Summary available: Health Department Research Findings No.6/2005

Enhancing Sexual Wellbeing in Scotland – A Sexual Health and Relationship Strategy: Analysis of Non – Written Responses to the Public Consultation: Dr Cathy Sharp (Research for Real). (2005) (£5.00)
Summary available: Health Department Research Findings No.6/2005

Research on Approaches to Public Funding and Development of Tertiary Education within Selected OECD Nations: Professor Michael Osborne (Centre for Research in Lifelong Learning) and Professor David Bell (Scotecon, University of Stirling). (2005) (Web only)
Summary available: Enterprise and Lifelong Learning Research Findings No.10/2005

Enterprise in Education: SME Survey: TNS System Three. (2005) (£5.00)
Summary available: Enterprise and Lifelong Learning Research Findings No.21/2005

Cross-Jurisdictional Comparison of Legal Provisions for Unmarried Cohabiting Couples: Sarah Bulloch and Debbie Headrick (Legal Studies Research Team, Scottish Executive). (2005) (Free)
Summary only available: Legal Studies Research Findings No.55/2005

Scottish Court Service User Satisfaction Survey 2004: Progressive Partnership. (2005) (£5:00)

Maintaining Houses – Preserving Homes: A Report on Responses to the Consultation: Robert Stevenson, Jim Patton and Rosemary Brotchie (Hexagon Research & Consulting). (2005) (Web only)
Summary available: Development Department Research Findings No 199/2005

Analysis of Responses to the Consultation on Existing Provisions and Licensing Arrangements of the Anatomy Act 1984: Linda Nicholson (The Research Shop). (2005) (£5.00)
Summary available: Health Department Research Findings No.2/2005

Retention of Organs at Post-Mortem: Analysis of Responses to the Consultation on the Review Group Phase 3 Report: Linda Nicholson (The Research Shop). (2005) (£5.00)
Summary available: Health Department Research Findings No.3/2005

Legislation Relating to Organ and Tissue Donation and Transplantation: Analysis of Consultation Responses: Linda Nicholson (The Research Shop). (2005) (£5.00)
Summary available: Health Department Research Findings No.4/2005

Legislation Relating to Hospital Post-Mortem Examinations: Analysis of Consultation Responses: Linda Nicholson (The Research Shop). (2005) (£5.00)
Summary available: Health Department Research Findings No.5/2005

Competitive Scottish Cities? Placing Scotland's Cities in the UK and European Context: Mary Hutchins and Michael Parkinson (European Institute for Urban Affairs, Liverpool John Moores University). (2005) (£5.00)

Improving the Collection of Volunteering Data in Scotland: Robert Stevenson (RDS Consulting (now part of Hexagon Research & Consulting)). (2005) (Web only).

Scottish Credit Unions – Meeting Member Demands and Needs: Keith Hayton, Lorraine Gray and Karen Stirling (GEN Consulting). (2005) (£5.00)
Summary available: Social Justice Research Findings No.16/2005

Anti-Social Behaviour on Buses: Sue Granville and Diarmid Campbell-Jack (George Street Research Limited). (2005) (Web only)
Summary available: Development Department Research Findings No.196/2005

Development of Tools to Measure Service User and Carer Satisfaction with Single Shared Assessment: Infusion Co-operative Limited. (2005) (Web only)

Columba 1400: Head Teacher Leadership Academy: Professor David Deakins, Dr Keith Glancey, Janette Wyper (Paisley Enterprise Research Centre, University of Paisley) and Professor Ian Menter (Faculty of Education, University of Glasgow). (2005) (Web only)
Summary available: Enterprise and Lifelong Learning Research Findings No.18/2005 (Web only)

Final Evaluation of the Rough Sleepers Initiative: Suzanne Fitzpatrick, Nicholas Pleace and Mark Bevan (Centre for Housing Policy, University of York). (2005) (£5.00)
Summary available: Development Department Research Findings No.200/2005

Social Inclusion Research Bulletin No. 13/2005: (2005) (Free)

Methodology for Assessing the Implications of Expanding Priority Need: Valerie Strachan, Laurie Naumann, Chris Adams, Jane Elrick and Francesca Richards (Tribal HCH). (2005) (£5.00)
Summary available: Development Department Research Findings No.197/2005

Operation of Power to Modify Local Connection Provisions: Valerie Strachan, Laurie Naumann, Chris Adams and Jane Elrick (Tribal HCH). (2005) (£5.00)
Summary available: Development Department Research Findings No.198/2005

The National Evaluation of the Careers Scotland Inclusiveness Projects: SQW Ltd. (2005) (Web only)
Summary available: Enterprise and Lifelong Learning Research Findings No.22/2005

Supported Employment for Young People Pilot: SQW Limited. (2005) (Web only)
Summary available: Enterprise and Lifelong Learning Research Findngs No.23/2005 (Web only)

Evaluation of the All Age Guidance Projects: SQW with TNS. (2005) (Web only)
Summary available: Enterprise and Lifelong Learning Research Findings No.24/2005 (Web only)

Monitoring and Evaluation of the Scottish Compact Baseline Results 2004: Keith Hayton, Loraine Gray and Karen Stirling (GEN Consulting). (2005) (£5.00)
Summary available: Social Justice Research Findings No.17/2005

Effective Community Involvement in Planning: PPS Local and Regional Limited. (2005) (Web only)

Resident Survey of the Dundee Home Zone: Land Use Consultants. (2005) (Web only).

Determined to Succeed: Investigating Young People's Perceptions of Success and Influencing Factors: Adam C Henderson (TNS System Three). (2005) (Web only)
Summary avaiilable: Office of Chief Researcher Research Findings No.9/2005 (Web only)

Determined to Succeed: Benchmarking Research of Children and Young People's Perceptions of Enterprise: Lee Langford and Carmen Aitken (Synovate). (2005) (Web only)
Summary available: Office of Chief Researcher Research Findings No.10/2005

Health For All Children: Guidance on Implementation in Scotland - Analysis of Consultation Responses: Reid Howie Associates. (2005) (Web only)
Summary available: Health Department Research Findings No.7/2005 (Web only)

Assessing the Effectiveness of Variable Messaging Signs to Inform Beach Users about Bathing Water Quality: MRUK. (2005) (Web only)
Summary available: Office of Chief Researcher Research Findings No.8/2005 (Web only)

Funding for Learners Review: Funding Available to Learners in Tertiary Education – An International Comparison: Scottish Executive Enterprise, Transport and Lifelong Learning Department. (2005) (Web only)
Summary available: Enterprise and Lifelong Learning Research Findings No.26/2005

Education Maintenance Allowances (EMAs) Attainment of National Qualifications in the Scottish Pilots: Linda Croxford, Jenny Ozga and Frances Provan (Centre for Educational Sociology, University of Edinburgh). (2005) (£5:00)
Summary available: Enterprise and Lifelong Learning Research Findings No.25/2005

Scottish Executive Education Department Communications Strategy Research: TNS Sytem Three. (2005) (Web only)
Summary available: Office of Chief Research Research Findings No.11/2005 (Web only)

Investigation of Access to Public Services in Scotland using British Sign Language: Jim Kyle, Anna Marie Reilly, Lorna Allsop, Monica Clark and Alexy Dury (Deaf Studies Trust). (2005) (£5.00)
Summary available: Social Justice Research Findings No.18/2005

An Evaluation of the Care in Scotland Campaign Wave 3: March 2004: TNS System Three. (2005) (Web only)

Evaluation of the Colinton All Postal Vote By–Election Pilot Scheme: Bob Jack and MORI Scotland. (2005) (Web only)

Communities That Care: An Evaluation of the Scottish Pilot Programme: Jon Bannister and Jennifer Dillane (University of Glasgow). (2005) (Free)
Summary only available: Criminal Justice Research Findings No.79/2005

Changing to Deliver Evaluation: (2005) (Free)
Summary only available: Office of Chief Researcher Research Findings No. 12/2005 (Web only)

Annual Survey of Small Businesses Scotland 2003: Fiona Neathey, Jennifer Hurtsfield, Becci Newton, Peter Bates (Institute for Employment Studies). (2005) (£5:00)
Summary available: Enterprise and Lifelong Learning Research Findngs No.27/2005

Household Survey of Entrepreneurship 2003: Nick Moon, Claire Ivins, Samantha Spencer (NOP Social & Political). (2005) (Web only)
Summary available: Enterprise and Lifelong Learning Research Findngs No.28/2005

"Go For It": Supporting People with Learning Disabilities and/or Autistic Spectrum Disorders in Employment: Julie Ridley, Susan Hunter and Infusion Cooperative (2005) (£5.00)
Summary available: Health and Community Care Research Findings No.45/2005

Evaluation of the Hamilton Sheriff Youth Court Pilot 2003-2005: Frank Popham, Gill McIvor, Alison Brown, Susan Eley, Margaret Malloch, Cathy Murray, Laura Piacentini, Reece Walters (Department of Applied Social Science University of Stirling) and Lorraine Murray (TNS Social). (2005) (£5:00)
Summary available: Crime and Criminal Justice Research Findings No.80

Minority Ethnic Enterprise in Scotland: Professor David Deakins, Dr Mohammad Ishaq, Geoff Whittam, Janette Wyper (Paisley Enterprise Research Centre, University of Paisley) and Professor David Smallbone (Small Business Research Centre, Kingston). (2005) (£5.00)
Summary available: Social Justice Research Findings No.19/2005

Ethnic Identity and the Census: Susie Macdonald, Vanessa Stone (BMRB Social Research), Rowena Arshad (Centre for Education for Racial Equality in Scotland (CERES), University of Edinburgh) and Philomena de Lima (UHI Policy Web, UHI Millenium Institute). (2005) (£5.00)
Summary available: Social Justice Research Findings No.20/2005

Further information on any of the above is available by contacting:

Dissemination Officer
Scottish Executive
Office of Chief Researcher
4th Floor West Rear
St Andrew's House
Edinburgh EH1 3DG

Email: **socialresearch@scotland.gsi.gov.uk**

Or by accessing the World Wide Website:
http://www.scotland.gov.uk/socialresearch